CHOOSING THE PERFECT PUPPY

CHOOSING THE PERFECT PUPPY

EVERYTHING YOU NEED TO KNOW
TO FIND THE BEST PUP FOR YOU

PIPPA MATTINSON

EBURY
PRESS

1 3 5 7 9 10 8 6 4 2

Ebury Press, an imprint of Ebury Publishing,
20 Vauxhall Bridge Road,
London SW1V 2SA

Ebury Press is part of the Penguin Random House group of companies
whose addresses can be found at global.penguinrandomhouse.com

Penguin
Random House
UK

Photography © Nick Ridley 2017
with the exception of p.118 © Jessica Gilmore 2017

First published by Ebury Press in 2017

www.eburypublishing.co.uk

A CIP catalogue record for this book is available from the British Library

ISBN 9781785034374

Printed and bound in China by Toppan Leefung

Penguin Random House is committed to a sustainable
future for our business, our readers and our planet.
This book is made from Forest Stewardship Council® certified paper.

Contents

Pippa Mattinson is a zoologist and the founder of The Gundog Trust – the UK's first gundog training and welfare charity. She is a keen supporter of modern, science-based dog training methods, and is passionate about helping people to enjoy their dogs. Visit her website for more information: www.pippamattinson.com

Acknowledgements

Thank you to everyone who has made this book possible and supported me, with coffee and kind words, throughout. In particular I'd like to thank Lucy Easton for her help with research and data, and for ensuring the smooth running of our websites throughout this project, and Sammie Austwick for her help with balancing the content and structure of this book. Thanks also to Toby Mattinson and Tom Mattinson for their support and encouragement.

Thanks to my agent Christopher Little, to Emma Schlesinger and to Jules Bearman, for their valuable input and support. Thanks to Carey Smith and the team at Ebury for their patience, and enthusiasm. Thanks also to photographer Nick Ridley for providing so many beautiful images to choose from. My thanks as ever to my husband Duncan Mattinson, for his invaluable support, for taking care of our home, for making sure that dogs and humans were well fed, and for generally ensuring that life carried on around me while I immersed myself in this book.

Finally, my thanks to the veterinarians and other scientists mentioned here, and whose work enables us to make better choices. And to all those who campaign tirelessly for improvements in canine health and welfare.

Part One

What Makes a Perfect Puppy?

1

The Right Time

Most of us accept that owning a dog will change our lives, but many of us are not aware of just how different things will be once a puppy arrives. Even the smallest and least demanding of dogs will alter your everyday routine in some respect, and some dogs will disrupt your life in ways you may never have imagined. Living with a dog should be fun. Things will change, but they should change for the better. This is much more likely to happen if your puppy is a good match for your family and your lifestyle: both in terms of his personality and in the physical impact he has on your home. It is also

Puppy perfection, but are you ready?

more likely to happen if your puppy grows into a healthy dog who is around for at least the next decade – hopefully more. Not every type of dog is suited to every type of family; fortunately, there are many different breeds of dog to choose from.

But we also need to consider that not every family will be at a place in their life where a dog will bring them joy. There are both good and bad times to get a puppy. For that reason, I don't think we can really get down to the important business of finding that perfect puppy until we are quite sure that right here, and right now, is a good time for you to bring a puppy into your life.

So, let's just spend a few minutes looking at what is involved in owning a dog generally, and at what a small puppy will need from you over the next few weeks and months if he is to grow into a well-adjusted and likeable adult dog.

How owning a dog will change your life

Puppies grow up very quickly, and you'll soon have a fully grown dog to share your home and leisure time with. We'll begin by looking at how life with an *adult* dog will be different from the life you have now. Then we'll look at the financial costs of raising a puppy, but keeping a dog doesn't just affect your bank balance. A dog eats into the hours in your day and burrows into your heart, and we'll look at the emotional cost and the demands on your time, too.

We'll also consider the impact a dog can make on your home and garden. Some dogs take great pleasure in digging, and if yours is an excavator, you can end up with a yard that looks more like a lunar landscape than a pretty garden. There are ways around this, but they usually involve money, effort, or a combination of the two. There will be some changes indoors too. Like babies, dogs come with their own paraphernalia, and not everyone is comfortable with the hair, and mess, that comes as part of the package with some of the larger, shedding breeds.

The financial costs of keeping a dog

People often ask how much they will need to pay for a puppy of this breed or that breed. But the initial cost of buying a puppy is almost insignificant compared with the costs involved in looking after him in the long term. This is especially true of some of the less healthy breeds. Some routine costs you might want to consider are health insurance, boarding or pet-sitting fees and food.

Unless you have very deep pockets you will need to insure your dog against medical problems. Modern veterinary treatments are amazing, but they can be extremely expensive. An operation to repair cruciate ligament damage (knee injuries) in a Labrador, for example, could set you back by several thousand pounds/dollars. Buying a good pet health insurance policy can take the pain out of paying the vet if your dog gets sick, but it will make a dent in your monthly salary.

If you want to holiday without your dog, you will need to factor boarding kennel fees or pet-sitting into the cost of your annual vacation.

Good-quality dog food isn't cheap, and obviously a larger dog will cost rather more to feed than a small one.

Where costs can really mount up is for those who are raising a dog while holding down a full-time job. Most dogs simply cannot be left alone all day, every day. I am often asked questions by concerned dog owners about problems they are having with their dog while they are at work, and these are difficulties caused

A puppy changes your life in many different ways.

by long hours of isolation. In many cases, these are serious issues that the owner hadn't anticipated. Apart from the fact that the dog needs access to a toilet area, he also needs company, and many dogs will become very destructive or noisy if left alone for long periods of time. So if you work, you will probably need to pay for some form of doggy daycare.

A major, initial cost for some families, when bringing home their first dog, is fencing. Many new dog owners do not realise that adult dog won't necessarily 'hang around' the homestead in the absence of a boundary or supervision. You can't expect a puppy or even an older dog to respect invisible boundaries, or to have any understanding of traffic and the need to avoid it. If you haven't done so already, you will probably need to secure your backyard or garden, or build some kind of secure outdoor run for your dog to use for bathroom purposes. Fencing contractors can be expensive, so if you are able to do this work yourself you will save a lot of money.

Most of the other costs involved in owning a dog are less significant. You can, of course, spend a fortune on dog sofas and fancy duvets, but these are not essential. Your dog will be just as happy snoozing on an old blanket in a basket on the floor, or relaxing on your sofa if you don't mind the hairs.

Of course there are many benefits to owning a dog, and many pleasures in store for you when you bring a dog into your life. If owning a dog means you can no longer afford to eat out in fancy restaurants, your long walks together may more than make up for that. And the joy of having a dog sleep by your feet each evening may be more than enough to help you give up one of your two annual holidays. But only you can make that decision, and you do need to be confident that the benefits you anticipate will stand a reasonable chance of outweighing any loss of enjoyment you may suffer in other respects. It is well worth spending a few minutes sitting down with a pen and paper and adding up just how much your new friend is going to add to your monthly bills.

The emotional costs of owning a dog

The emotional benefits of owning a dog are widely recognised. We place great value on the companionship, affection and loyalty that dogs give to their families. But there are costs to consider as well. Most people get deeply attached to their dogs and miss them when they are apart. For many of us, owning a dog means an end to some of the carefree activities we used to enjoy before dog ownership came along. Not just because we may have to pay someone to care for our dog when we go trekking in the Himalayas, but because we would miss him too much to really enjoy it.

While there are things you can do to help make sure your puppy is healthy, well behaved and lives a long life, there are no guarantees. Dogs may get sick and need nursing, or have ongoing health problems. And because we love them, we worry about them. Some dogs have behavioural issues, and some of these can have a major impact on your family. Dogs grow old all too soon and eventually leave us, and we mourn them. All these eventualities can turn your life upside down.

For most of us, these costs are a worthwhile price to pay for years of friendship and joy, but if your life is *already* tough, more things to worry about and care about might just be too much for you *at the moment*. Responsibility is stressful and loving means hurting sometimes. Bringing more love and more responsibility into your life is best undertaken when your own life is on an even keel. That way you will be able to offer your dog your full attention, and give him the love and care that he needs.

The demands a dog will make on your time

Spending time with a dog can and should be one of the great joys in life. All adult dogs place some demands on your time, because they need feeding, exercise and a certain amount of company. Puppies place quite *heavy* demands on your time because they need to be toilet trained, obedience trained, socialised, and because they need *a lot* of your company and attention if they are to thrive and be well adjusted.

One of the biggest time commitments in owning a dog is exercise, and training is a close second. There are dogs that don't need much exercise, but unfortunately they tend to come with serious health problems. We'll be looking more closely at that later on. Essentially, healthy dogs need to walk and run every single day, rain or shine. This can be a great thing for you if you are ready for it. Many people have become very fit as a result. It makes sense, though, to ensure you will have the time to exercise your dog morning and evening.

Dogs, even little dogs, should not be shut indoors alone all day. If you intend to come home at midday to exercise and play with your dog, don't forget to factor in the journey time as well as the time you spend with him. Some people anticipate that they will see to their dog in their lunchbreak, but find it much harder than they anticipated. Do some dummy runs *before* you get your puppy to make sure this is something you'll be able to cope with. It's also a good idea to make sure you can actually bear getting up an hour earlier each day to walk and train your dog before work. It is harder to do than it is to say.

Training takes time and commitment. People often write to me and say that their puppy doesn't 'listen' or doesn't like them. By this they mean that they give the puppy instructions and he ignores them. This is normal behaviour in puppies. We need to teach puppies the kinds of behaviour we want from them and help them learn to respond to the right cues or commands. With small puppies, this takes only a few minutes two or three times a day, but as your puppy grows you will need to teach him to respond to your commands outdoors and in different locations. This can be time consuming, because it often involves travelling and getting help from other people. Most new puppy owners will need to join a dog training class to get their dogs to a good standard of obedience.

Modern dog training is actually a huge amount of fun, and for many of us the daily dog walks and training sessions are some of the best moments of the day. They only become a problem when we simply don't have the time required to devote to them, so it is worth scheduling this in in advance.

The way a dog will change your home

Dogs can be very messy. Especially larger, hairier dogs. And some dogs have a distinctive body odour that doesn't appeal to everyone. If your home is immaculate, it is definitely worth asking yourself if you are ready to let your standards slip, just a little. Will you mind if the rooms where your dog spends much of his time are dustier, muddier and hairier than before?

If your home is already a bit chaotic, you may think a dog won't make any difference. But keeping a dog in a messy home can be a challenge, too, especially dogs that chew a lot and love to carry things around.

Your backyard or garden is likely to be a place where your dog will spend some of his time. Depending on the breed, and the individual dog, this can have quite an impact on your landscaping. If you are a keen gardener, you may need to consider making some adjustments to your garden area. You might find it helpful to provide a special toilet area to protect your lawn. Fencing off a puppy play area and providing a sandbox for him to dig in will help keep your lawn and flowerbeds safe, while you wait for your puppy to outgrow the destructive stage.

This might seem like a lot of trouble to go to, but being well prepared can make the whole experience a lot more fun.

The special needs of a puppy

A puppy's needs are somewhat different from those of an older dog. Obviously, your puppy will grow into a dog quite quickly, but for a while he will be quite demanding of your time and attention. You have to be confident that you can either provide for his needs during the next few weeks, or pay someone else to do that for you. Asking for someone to care for a puppy as a favour is unlikely to work out for more than a few days, unless they really owe you one!

Puppies, like babies, can interfere with your sleep and impose demands on you that can make you feel stressed and irritable. This isn't anything you won't be able to cope with, provided you are not already under a lot of stress for different reasons, but it is something to bear in mind when you are choosing the right time to get a puppy. The most time-consuming tasks that face the new puppy owner are socialisation and housetraining, and most of the effort you'll need to put into these tasks has to be squashed into the first couple of months.

Puppies all need to be socialised. We tend to think of dogs as being naturally friendly, but actually this isn't strictly true. Dogs that are deprived of social experiences during early puppyhood become extremely fearful of anything unusual, and this can lead to aggression. This means that new puppies need to meet lots of new people and be placed in lots of new situations. Socialisation is time consuming but it can be very enjoyable. It isn't difficult to achieve in a busy sociable family; those living in more isolated situations will have to work harder at it.

Housetraining is another process that needs a lot of input from you, or from a substitute provided by you. Puppies can only last a very short time without bathroom breaks for those first few weeks, and though you can teach your puppy to empty himself on puppy pads or newspaper, it is very helpful if someone is present to help your puppy pee and poop in the right place from the very beginning.

You'll also need someone to be around partway through the day to feed your little one. Your puppy will need to be fed four times a day for the first three months, then three times a day until he is six months old. You can't just divide his rations into two and give them to him before and after work, because puppies get upset tummies if given too much food at one time.

Most importantly, puppies need company. A well-adjusted adult dog will be happy to be left alone for stretches of time. But to get to that point he needs to have an appropriate upbringing. Puppies that are isolated for long periods may be noisy or destructive. They may also become fearful of being left, which can cause long-term problems including soiling, howling and destructive behaviour, not to mention great distress to the dog.

Puppies are hugely appealing and they fulfil a very basic human need to love and be loved. Yet despite their appeal, the idea of bringing such a vulnerable and helpless little creature into your life can be daunting. If you are feeling apprehensive at this point, that is not such a bad thing. If you are worried about the responsibility of owning a dog, it shows that you are taking that responsibility seriously, and suggests that you may well be just the right person to give a dog a loving home.

Raising a puppy while you work

Holding down a full-time job and raising a contented and well-adjusted dog are not mutually exclusive. Many people do it. But if this is what you are hoping to do, you will need to plan in advance because you will need help. Most people that work away from home take a few weeks off to coincide with the arrival of their puppy. This, together with some form of daycare once you return to the office, can work well.

During the very early weeks, your puppy will need plenty of company and socialisation outings. He'll also need to be taught how to be alone for short periods of time by people who understand, or are willing to learn, the principles of basic puppy training.

It is well worth finding out in advance of buying your puppy what kind of daycare facilities or professional dog walkers are available in your area – find out exactly what their terms and condition are, and what daycare will cost you on a weekly basis. The terms and conditions will specify at what age they will take your puppy. Not many will take a pup before he has completed his full course of vaccinations, or before he is three or four months old; they may also specify whether or not your dog must be neutered and at what age.

If you need to go back to work before the daycare centre can take your puppy, you'll need help from a willing friend, neighbour or family member to spend time with him each day, taking him out and about, and helping with potty training.

You are also likely to be returning to work before your puppy can last more than a couple of hours without a wee, so you'll need to use the paper training methods of housetraining. This means that you will need to provide your puppy with a large sturdy playpen lined with puppy pads or newspaper, or to provide a puppy-proof room to keep your little one safe from hazards while he is alone.

Once he is older, you may be able to replace daycare and help from friends and neighbours with a daily midday visit and exercise from a dog walker. If you cannot arrange these things, then you are likely to struggle.

Picking the right time to get a puppy

If you are confident your family is ready for a puppy, it's a good idea to think about the best time to bring your puppy home. Avoid major life-changing events and large family celebrations if you can. In many cases it is easier to cope with a puppy – especially with night-time toilet trips – in the warmer summer months, and fortunately this coincides with the time of year that the majority of puppies are born.

Raising a puppy and a baby together might seem like a great idea and a good way to capitalise on maternity leave, but it can be harder than you think. The puppy and the baby will each have their own separate needs, which will pull your heartstrings in different directions and might leave you feeling frazzled. Raising a puppy when you have a toddler around can be challenging, too. Small puppies bite very hard and half-grown puppies are very clumsy, especially with some of the larger, bouncier breeds. Toddlers can end up spending half the time flat on their faces while the puppy scampers around them, and the other half in tears because the puppy is chewing their toes.

Ideally, you need to be able to focus on your puppy for those first few weeks and to enjoy his puppyhood, which is all too short.

SUMMARY

- I have spent a little time exploring how a dog will change your life, not to put you off owning a dog, but to help ensure you are in the right place to set off on this wonderful journey of discovery. One way to find out if you are ready is to borrow a friend's dog and look after it for a few days. You'll hopefully enjoy the early morning walks, discover how you feel about a dog's presence in your home, and your friend will enjoy a few lie ins. If more people did this, I am convinced that there would be far fewer dogs in shelters.
- The next step is to make sure that you are matched with the right type of dog. A dog that will fit in with your way of life, and bring joy and happiness into your home. If you are confident that you are ready for what lies ahead, it's time to start looking for your new best friend.

2
So Much Choice

The variety of different breeds and crossbreeds of dog that we have created in the last hundred years or so is nothing short of breathtaking, and choosing between them is quite a challenge in itself. You may have a pretty good idea already of the type of dog you want to bring home, or you may be completely bewildered by the choice and variety available to you. Perhaps you are undecided whether or not to buy a puppy from a breeder, or whether to try to rescue one from a shelter. Maybe you are unsure whether or not a purebred dog is a good idea, even though you like them. Perhaps you fancy a designer dog but are worried that there could be risks involved; such dogs might have poor temperaments, or be unhealthy. These are all issues we are going to tackle in this book.

There are a lot of different puppy breeds to choose from.

I'll begin by looking at what draws us to particular breeds or types of dog, and why it may be important to research more deeply, and perhaps step outside our comfort zones, before making up our minds. We'll also look at the different roles that dogs play in our society. We'll explore how the wider role of dogs as human companions has changed over the last hundred years or so, and at how those changes have created the bewildering diversity of dogs you see today. I'll also help you to think with your head a little, because choosing a puppy with your heart alone can lead to trouble.

Following your heart

What makes people attracted to one dog over another? Why do some of us have our heart set on a Golden Retriever and nothing else will do? Why do some of us find the Bulldog so appealing, while others are convinced their lives will never be complete until there is a St Bernard on their couch.

Very often these attractions have their roots in our childhood. Dogs we remember from when we were little, family dogs, nice dogs, and nasty ones too, all make an impression which influences our future choices. And, of course, each generation has its own canine media heroes, dogs that appear in feature films, books, newspapers or children's television. From Lassie the Rough Collie, a television superstar in the 1950s, to Winston the Boston Terrier in the animated film *Feast*, dogs in popular culture have always enchanted children and adults alike. Celebrity dog owners can be a powerful influence too.

Sometimes a dog with a particular appearance is favoured for reasons that are more fundamentally human. Young animals are particularly attractive as they evoke our maternal and paternal instincts. Over the generations, we have bred some dogs with shorter snouts, floppy ears and bigger eyes, and these baby-like features have been shown to be very appealing to many of us. You may of course ask, What is the problem with simply following your heart and choosing a puppy based on what appeals to you? Let's have a look.

All dogs are not equal

When we buy a car or a refrigerator, we often scour the internet for reviews first. We know that some cars are more dependable, more long-lived than others. And we know that some fridges are much more likely to stop working in the first year. These are expensive purchases, so we do our homework. But with dogs, many of us rush out to buy the first one we come across.

There is a natural reluctance to make intrusive enquiries into the background of a living thing. You may have been told that you need to check health certificates for the parents of your puppy, but you wouldn't grill a future spouse on the diseases their uncles suffered from or on the behaviour of their mothers and fathers, so why would you do so with a dog?

'My dog is not a fridge!' you cry, and rightly so. However, unlike your spouse, your future dog is almost definitely a purchase, and one which involves a contract of sale, even if no paper exchanges hands. A dog is also a purchase for which you are legally and morally responsible for the rest of his life. Most important of all, your future dog's happiness is at least partly dependent on his health, so if it is possible to influence that, then you owe him to put a little time and effort into your search.

Perhaps the most frequent reason that people buy puppies on impulse is because they are unaware that there are risks in doing so. They may believe that the term 'pedigree' carries with it some guarantee of good health or that dogs are all essentially equal in pretty much every respect. Their assumption is that health is generally a question of taking good care of your dog, together with a generous portion of good luck. Sadly, this is not the case.

While all dogs may be equally valuable and special, dogs are not equal when it comes to health and (perhaps more controversially) temperament. Nor is every dog equally suited to every family. There are in fact large differences between the health and longevity of different dog breeds, and some of our most popular dogs come with a lot of baggage.

You may not be aware, for example, that some breeds have a life expectancy of just five or six years, while others may live *three times as long*. Many new puppy buyers have no idea that some types of dog have severe problems just breathing and cooling themselves. This startling fact, and others like it, are often swept under the carpet when pedigree dogs are being discussed, yet there is a mountain of evidence and literature to confirm that they are true. In other words, your choice of puppy will help to decide whether your dog is likely to have a long and fun-filled life, or a troubled and short one. It's quite a responsibility.

When we consider the impact a dog has on your life, it makes sense to exercise your right to choose one with a healthy future. But you can only do that if you put some thought and planning into purchasing your new friend. Luck should not feature anywhere in this decision.

❧ The diversity of dogs and how that diversity arose

Most of the time, when two animals are strikingly different in appearance, it is because they belong to different species, and have evolved for different roles or to take advantage of different environmental niches on our complex planet. This general rule falls apart when it comes to domesticated animals. The protection offered them by mankind has freed them from the forces of natural selection. Once an animal does not have to fight for survival, some interesting and varied body types are free to appear. Nowhere is this more apparent than it is in our modern-day dogs.

When we look at the massive Newfoundland or Great Dane and compare them with the tiny Chihuahua or the Shih Tzu, it is hard to believe that our giant dogs came from exactly the same ancestors as their miniature cousins. Although we now know through DNA testing that our domestic dogs are all directly descended from the grey wolf, generations of selective breeding have created the vast diversity of dogs that we see today. The origins of much of this diversity lie in the different roles we created for our dogs.

🐾 The changing role of the dog

When humans first began to influence the structure and the temperament of the dogs they shared their lives with, it was largely to improve those dogs for the roles they had in mind. We kept dogs to guard us, help us hunt, herd and protect our livestock, and to keep us company. And we began to select the dogs that performed the best at these jobs and to breed them with other suitably able dogs.

Early dogs would have been general hunting companions, capable of helping to pull down prey and willing to help protect their families. Later, as man moved from hunter gatherer communities to agricultural settlements, and to hunt for sport as well as necessity, the diversity of dog roles increased. Pack hunting dogs were bred for their amazing scenting ability, their capacity to run for long distances, and to kill, or hold their prey at bay until their human partners caught up and finished the job for them. Dogs intended to care for livestock were bred for both their herding and their guarding abilities. From tiny dogs that could run inside a turnspit, to powerful dogs that would fight one another to the death, there was no shortage of inspiration for the new roles man dreamed up for his best friend.

Because we were living in such close proximity to these powerful predators, it was also important that only dogs that were friendly towards family members were bred from. As soon as humans took over the decisions about which dogs would breed, and began selecting dogs for docility as well as ability, a whole range of other characteristics that would never have had the chance to be expressed in their wolf ancestors began to appear. A fascinating study of wild foxes began in Russia in the 1950s and shows us how the variety we see in our modern dogs may have started quite early on when wolves were first domesticated. The foxes in the Russian experiment were captured and selectively bred on the basis of their friendliness or docility. The experiment ran for many decades and many of the features we see in domestic dogs appeared in these foxes within just a few

Some breeds need more grooming than others.

generations. Floppy ears, curly tails and different coat colours all rapidly appear when animals are selected for docility rather than survival. This variety may or may not have been important to our Stone Age ancestors, but as our urban society has developed, we have become increasingly interested in the appearance of our canine friends.

From function to form

Society's attitude towards dogs has changed immensely in the last 150 years. With that change has come a shift in our priorities with regard to the kind of dogs we want to share our lives with. With a few exceptions, we are no longer concerned with speed, agility, tracking ability or courage. We are now much more focused on appearance and general temperament. You probably don't intend to rely on your dog to help you catch your supper, or guard your sheep. Nor, I suspect, are you intending to keep him to bait bulls or fight other dogs to the death. We have a gentler purpose for our dogs these days.

However, it is only human nature to want to compete with others, and it is certain that 'who owns the best dog' has long been a topic of conversation around our hearths. Since the need to make dogs earn their keep has subsided in most parts of the world, most of us no longer compare or compete with our dogs in terms of performance or ability. Instead, we have found another way to match dogs against one another and win accolades for the best dog. That way is of course the show ring, and exhibiting dogs is a hugely popular pastime in our modern world.

The rise of dog fancy

The first ever dog show took place in 1859 in Newcastle, England. Field trials, or competitions to assess Gundogs, arose around the same time, but interest in shows soon eclipsed the sporting activities of the rural community and were appealing to a much wider section of society. For the first time, dogs were being judged and, more importantly, *selected for breeding* on the basis of their appearance rather than on their performance in the role for which they were originally intended. This was to have a far-reaching effect on the structure of some of our future pedigree dogs.

For a while, dogs were grouped into breeds or types by the jobs they did and by the way that their owners described them. If you called your dog a Spaniel, and used him for flushing game, then he was to all intents and purposes a Spaniel. People often kept records of the animals they bred so that they could learn from their experiences and improve on things the next time around. It was not a very big leap to formalise this record keeping nationally.

The development of pedigree registers

The separation of dogs into individual pedigree breeds, and the isolation of those breeds genetically, began in the late 1800s. The Kennel Club was formed on 4 April 1873 by a group of 13 British men led by Sewallis Shirley. The aim of the club was to ensure that dog shows and field trials were run fairly. The club also began keeping birth records of individual dogs within each of the popular breeds, and published their first monthly register of dog names in 1880. As time progressed, once each dog breed was recognised by the Kennel Club, and the names of the individual dogs within that breed listed on their register, the registers were closed, and crossbreeding between the breeds was outlawed. The aim was to produce a pure strain of dogs that bred true to type, generation after generation.

No one then could possibly have anticipated the significance of that step. At that point in time, all the genetic material that would *ever* be available to that particular breed of dog was contained within the register for that breed. The 'purebred' pedigree dog had arrived.

What a pedigree certificate can't tell us

It wasn't long before the terms purebred and pedigree took on a significance and status that made them sought after. Owning a pedigree dog was for many years a symbol of quality and prestige. Things have changed a little in the last few years. You will doubtless have heard some of the arguments currently raging about the health of pedigree dogs, and we'll be taking a look at the health of some of these breeds later in the book. For puppy buyers, there is sometimes confusion over what a Kennel Club pedigree can tell you about a puppy, and I think it is important to address this first.

A while ago, I was chatting to a friend I hadn't seen for some time and they were delighted to tell me that they would soon be collecting their new pedigree puppy. The dog was from a breed known to suffer from a particular type of heart condition that can lead to exercise intolerance, fainting and even death. This disease is detectable through a screening programme and all breeding stock from that breed needs to be tested before mating, in order to ensure no puppies in a litter can develop the disease as they grow. Not only had my friend *not* asked the breeder of his puppy if its parents had been tested, he had no idea that such a question was necessary. 'Don't worry,' he said to me, 'I've seen the pedigree.'

Like so many new puppy buyers, he had assumed that his puppy's pedigree certificate was proof that the puppy's parents were fit for breeding. Sadly, this is not the case at the present time. Anyone can register a litter of pedigree puppies provided they meet the Kennel Club's requirements with regard to the registration of the parents and the age and number of litters previously born to the mother.

We'll look later at the various health screening certificates that you'll need to check up on when you are purchasing a puppy. These vary from breed to breed, but, for now, it is very important to be aware that a pedigree certificate in isolation is not evidence of good health.

So are crossbreeds best?

But while a pedigree may not be a promise or guarantee of good health or good breeding, rushing out to buy a crossbreed isn't necessarily the answer. Being crossbred or of mixed breeding isn't a guarantee of health either. But don't worry! We'll be going into this topic in more detail and looking at the pros and cons of buying a pedigree dog compared with a mixed-breed dog in Chapter 6. There is a great deal of information in this book to help make sure that you don't end up with a puppy who has avoidable health problems.

SUMMARY

Aside from health, the other most important feature of your dog is his temperament. In the next chapter I will give you some tips on how you can influence this, not only by the breed of dog you choose, but also by choosing the breeder carefully, and by simple actions you can take when you bring your puppy home.

Choosing a healthy body for your puppy will help him to enjoy life.

3

The Right Temperament

Most Gundog breeds are friendly and easy to train.

The temperament of any dog has the potential to affect his life, and the lives of those around him, more profoundly than most new puppy buyers could ever imagine. No one ever notices the dogs that have a wonderful nature, because this is what we expect from a dog. Owning a dog of uncertain disposition can pervade every aspect of his family's life, whereas owning a dog with the right personality for a companion dog will bring endless pleasure to all those who come into contact with him. This is what we are going to help you to achieve. We'll look at what we mean by good temperament, at the factors that influence it, and at how you can improve your chances of bringing a friendly, confident puppy into your life.

Later, in Chapter 7, we'll look at some of the differences in personality between the different breed groups. But let's begin by defining exactly what we expect from a good-natured dog.

What do we mean by 'good temperament'?

We all have different expectations of a dog, but, for most of us, a dog with a good temperament is one that moves comfortably in human circles and is unruffled by the hustle and bustle of our urban world. He gets along well with adults, children and other dogs. He is friendly towards strangers and tolerant of being stroked, cuddled and fussed over. He rides happily in cars, boats and trains, and doesn't fear the hiss of a lorry's air brakes or the clang of unfamiliar machinery. He isn't inclined to obsessively chase joggers, vehicles or livestock, and he greets the postman with a wagging tail.

It sounds fairly simple, but, sadly, many pet dogs fail to meet these standards and, as a result, some are abandoned even before their first birthday. Every day I read sad emails from people whose dogs' behaviour is ruining their lives, and the comments on my website and the posts on my forum are full of questions from owners whose dogs embarrass or even frighten them. It doesn't need to be like this. There is much we can do, before you even meet him, to ensure that *your* dog is the dog that everyone would love to take home.

Why some dogs are unfriendly or aggressive

At one time, dangerous or aggressive dogs were thought to be born, rather than made. Dogs were often classified as 'mean' or 'friendly' by their breed alone. 'Don't go near the Alsatian' mother would say, while completely ignoring her toddler's attempt to cuddle an obviously irritated Labrador. Breed-specific legislation (BSL) was borne out of these beliefs in the inherited nature of aggression.

BSL involves the banning of specific breeds or types of dog, or placing conditions on who can own them and how they should be managed. Breed-specific legislation is hugely controversial because implicit within it is the assumption that certain types of dog are inherently more dangerous than others, and it involves making decisions about a dog's right to life based purely on his appearance.

Sweeping stereotypes are often wildly inaccurate, and assumptions about canine behaviour are no exception. Of course, not all Alsatians, or German Shepherd Dogs as they are now known, are guard dogs. And not all Labradors are friendly. But, today, the pendulum has swung in the opposite direction. There is currently widely expressed opinion among dog enthusiasts that dangerous dogs are a product of their environment, and a belief that all that is required to make any dog safe around people is the proper socialisation of puppies.

Now, socialisation is incredibly important, don't get me wrong. I write reams on how to socialise puppies and it is one of the most important processes you will ever go through with your dog. But to disregard breed as a factor in a dog's temperament is as foolish as to believe that socialisation is the answer to a perfect temperament in any dog. The truth lies, as it so often does, somewhere in the middle. Understanding the root causes of aggression is vital when you are about to enter the world of dog ownership, and we should be clear that both breed and environment play a part.

The most common contributory factor when it comes to aggression in dogs is fear. Dogs are afraid of the unfamiliar. This is where your role as your dog's carer and guardian come into play. The well-socialised family dog is unafraid because everything he meets is a part of the world he has grown up around. He isn't afraid of strangers because he has met hundreds of them and knows they are harmless. He isn't afraid of loud noises or the vacuum cleaner because it is just background noise to him. The world is his friend. But that isn't the end of the story.

Inherited temperament differences

Common sense tells us that behaviour characteristics must be inherited to *some* degree, or we would not have Sheepdogs that like to herd or Retrievers that like to retrieve. These are instinctive behaviours that come hardwired in many puppies of the relevant breed. Personality types are inherited too. If you buy a German Shepherd puppy, when he reaches the grand old age of three and you take him to the park, the chances of him greeting every passing stranger with a full body wag and offering them his favourite toy are slim. It could happen, but it isn't likely. And if your Jack Russell Terrier gets into a child's guinea pig pen, I wouldn't bet your paycheque on him giving them a little wash and snuggling down next to them for a nap, though it could happen. While it is clear that the tendency to behave in certain ways is inherited, with some breeds being naturally calmer, some more friendly and others more suspicious in nature, we cannot *rely* on behaviour to determine ancestry or on ancestry to predict behaviour.

Canine geneticist Carole Beuchat, from the Institute of Canine Biology, tells us that 'The heritability for most behavioural traits is rather low. This doesn't mean that genetics isn't important for behaviour, but that our ability to infer the genetics of an animal from observations of behaviour is limited because environmental factors produce so much variability that the fraction of total variation that can be attributed to genes is small.'

Dogs are individuals. We don't want all dogs to be pigeonholed according to their breed, or assumptions to be made that might affect a dog's future or safety to be based on their breed, which is why many people are campaigning to see breed-specific legislation abolished. However, we do need to recognise that some individual dogs are born with traits that may make them more or less suited to family life than other dogs. And that aggression towards other dogs, or towards people, may be more common in some breeds than in others.

Guarding behaviour in dogs

Some dogs have a natural guarding instinct. This is a natural instinct in wild canids like wolves. After all, if you don't guard your resources someone else is likely to take them. We have bred this guarding instinct out of many of our breeds, simply because a docile dog is easier and safer to handle. But in some breeds we have retained some instinct to guard so that our dogs can work on our behalf to protect property or livestock.

Guarding behaviour can occur in all dogs, but this behaviour is much stronger and more consistently found in certain breeds. Many of the breeds that belong to the Working group make formidable guard dogs, and some of our herding breeds, such as the Malinois, do too. Without protection-work training, many dogs from guarding breeds won't actually bite or attack people; the behaviour for many consists of posturing threats and lots of noise, warning people off, rather than a full-on attack. But, again, some breeds are more likely to bite than others if they feel threatened, some are less likely to give a warning before they bite, and others are less likely to let go of the person they have bitten, causing much more serious injuries.

Inappropriate guarding

Guarding or protecting behaviour is essentially borne out of suspicion. A dog that guards stuff suspects strangers of having dubious motives. This guarding behaviour can be incredibly useful and there is no doubt that in ancient times it was one of a dog's most valuable attributes. The problem with guarding behaviour lies in ensuring it is directed appropriately. This is very hard to do in the average family home.

It takes a significant structure to contain a large and determined dog, and to deter casual intruders. In most cases our backyards or gardens are not particularly secure. Innocent passers-by may be viewed as a threat to a dog with strong guarding instinct. It is also important to recognise that uninvited entry to your property is not necessarily indicative of evil intent.

Even if your property is secure, owning a dog with strong guarding tendencies is a big responsibility. Most dog attacks happen to family members or invited guests.

Kids climb over fences to retrieve a Frisbee or out of harmless mischief. Delivery people might look for somewhere to leave a parcel if you are out.

Ask yourself, who will supervise your guard dog and make sure that visitors are safe? Can you be absolutely certain that no passing child can ever squeeze through your hedge? Can you guarantee that no other family member will let the dog out while you are in the shower? Asking a dog to distinguish between those who mean harm and the mailman is probably a stretch too far. There is also provision for this kind of scenario within the law in many countries – if your dog causes injury, a sign on your gate that says 'beware of the dog' is no protection if you are sued. It is also worth bearing in mind that if your dog causes injury or is just reported as being aggressive he could be seized and destroyed.

As a puppy buyer, especially if we are also parents to small humans, we need to recognise that some dogs, should their temperament be less than perfect, have the potential to do far more harm than others.

Powerful dogs

All dogs, if frightened or harmed sufficiently, may eventually bite. But the truth is, some breeds are more likely to grow into large and powerful dogs that have a penetrating bite and don't let go once they have bitten. The average Cocker Spaniel does not have the strength to overpower and even kill a five-year-old child; the average Rottweiler does. A Pit Bull Terrier may be no more likely to bite than the Collie next door, but the Collie's bite is more likely to be a brief warning nip, whereas the Pit Bull is more likely to tear through muscle and bone. This does NOT mean that Rottweilers and Pit Bulls are all dangerous. It makes sense however to recognise that the different physical properties and behavioural traits of different breeds do impact on the potential of a badly raised individual dog to cause harm.

A safe companion

Despite the fact that most of us recognise the importance of a friendly dog, and the risks of being responsible for a powerful and aggressive dog, I still get a lot of queries from people who want a dog to 'guard' the home. There are those who want to buy a guarding breed and make sure that the dog behaves appropriately towards their family and friends. More commonly, there are those who buy a basically friendly breed and want to know how to turn him into a guard dog.

It is important to choose a breed with the right temperament.

- There is a serious conflict of interests here. My general view is that powerful dogs with strong guarding or protection instincts are best left to experienced dog handlers. If this is your first puppy, and you have small children, it makes sense to pick a breed that fits all or most of these criteria:

- Tends to be friendly or fairly indifferent towards strangers
- Tends to be tolerant of human behaviours
- Tends not to be very heavy and powerful
- Tends not to guard property or people
- Tends to warn (growl) before biting
- Tends to nip and let go if a bite occurs.

Again, there are no guarantees about individual dogs, but there are very many breeds where the majority of individual dogs meet *all* these criteria. A dog that meets none of them is a high-risk animal in the hands of an inexperienced person, and dog protection work is best left to experts. I understand the urge to choose a breed that will fulfil the dual role of both family companion and guard dog, but my honest advice, if you are worried about safety, is to buy a dog from a breed that meets the criteria above and invest in a good home-security system.

How to ensure your puppy has a great temperament

For a friendly dog, everyday life serves to confirm his confident opinion that the world is a wonderful place. Passing strangers stop to say hello and admire his happy face, to give him treats or a kindly pat. Everyone is pleased to see him; life is good.

For a nervous or unfriendly dog, everyday experiences often serve to confirm his opinion that life is not much fun. His grumpy behaviour means that he begins to be left out of some family outings, and his absence is such a relief that leaving him behind becomes the norm. Strangers and strange places become ever more scary, as his world effectively shrinks. Before too long he is no longer a part of the family, but one of those embarrassing awkward relatives with a problem that no one wants to talk about and everyone would rather forget.

You are looking for a dog that is easy to get along with, and fortunately there are plenty of breeds that fit the bill.

> You can increase your chances of owning a dog with a great temperament in the following ways:
>
> - Choose your puppy from a breed known to be friendly
> - Choose a knowledgeable and committed breeder
> - Socialise your puppy adequately.

Choosing a friendly breed lays the foundations for a good temperament. Choosing a knowledgeable and committed breeder builds on those foundations. Those who care for the puppy during the first four months of his life cement that good temperament with a thorough program of socialisation. The window for socialising a puppy is brief, as dogs are only naturally accepting of new experiences before the age of about four months. After that point they become fearful of the unknown. The role of your breeder is to ensure that your puppy's socialisation has already begun before he leaves his mother. Your job is to finish the process.

SUMMARY

We'll be returning to temperament in Chapter 7, when we look at the characteristics of different groups of dogs. But, for now, we are now going to shift our focus to health.

4

A Healthy Structure

We all want our dogs to be healthy, and not all puppies are born equal in this respect. A dog in poor health can impact on your whole family, not least because caring for a sick pet can be demanding, exhausting and expensive, but also because we love our dogs and want them to be happy.

There are health tests available for each of the various pedigree dog breeds, and you need to ask for evidence that these tests have been carried out before purchasing a puppy, but before you even begin to think about asking to see certificates of health, there is actually a range of much simpler assessments that you can first apply yourself to the breeds that appeal to you.

Health issues in dogs can be broadly divided into two: the problems we can see and those we can't. Health tests, which we'll be looking at in the next chapter, help identify the issues we cannot see. Health and structure are inextricably entwined. The problems we can see with our eyes are to do with the way some breeds of dog are constructed, specifically with how much the dog has been changed from the original canine blueprint that we can still see in our wild wolves today. This is what we are going to look at in this chapter.

The original structure of the dog

The wolf is a 'boxy' kind of animal. If you look at him from the side, the length of his front leg and his back leg is fairly proportional to the distance between them. These proportions dominate in the world of larger mammals because mechanically they make sense. Horses, deer, big cats, and other large animals capable of running at speed, tend to have this body structure with the length of leg matching the length of spine (excluding the tail) fairly closely. The main benefit of this shape is that it gives the spine adequate support and enables the animal to run and jump freely. Activity generates heat, of course, and unlike mammals that cool themselves through sweating, wolves have an efficient cooling system built right into their long muzzles, losing moisture along the surface of the mouth as they pant. They also have a dense water-repellent coat to retain body heat when at rest and in cool weather. Everything about the wolf – his size, colour, coat, skin, muscles, bones, and the relative proportions of his body parts to one another – is perfectly suited to survival in a demanding and sometimes inhospitable world. Dogs, on the other hand, share our world and no longer have need of many of the survival advantages that Mother Nature has bestowed on the wolf. So we have been able to change dogs in many ways to suit our needs and our enthusiasm for variety.

The impact of changing a dog's structure

From the original grey wolf blueprint, we have created dogs in many different forms. We have changed coat lengths and leg lengths, created giant dogs and tiny ones, curly tails and floppy ears, and a myriad different colours. Some of the things we have done to our dogs have had a fairly minimal impact on the animals concerned. Changes in coat length, density, texture or colour are not normally a problem for a well-groomed dog living in a centrally heated or air-conditioned home. Nor are changes in ear carriage or tail length – while floppy ears are more prone to infections, many floppy-eared dogs are still relatively healthy.

The big problem for dogs is that we have carried on making changes, *even* where those features carry a disadvantage to the dog. In recent decades, as the interest in exhibiting dogs has grown and become more competitive, some of those features that make our different breeds distinct from one another have become increasingly exaggerated.

To have a chance of raising a puppy to be a healthy dog, we need to begin with a dog that is well designed. You don't need to be an expert to see or hear the problems I'll cover here, all you need is to be aware that these features in any dog are a problem for the dog. There are nine of them altogether:

- Very short legs
- Twisted tails
- Closed or pinched nostrils
- Noisy breathing and excessive panting
- Very short muzzles
- Bulging eyes
- Skinfolds
- Banana backs
- Extremes of size

These aren't the only obvious problems that can arise from a poorly structured dog, but they are key issues to avoid if you are to find a truly healthy puppy. Let's start with what is possibly the most obvious problem of all – a set of very short legs.

Very short legs

Sometimes, dogs are born with various forms of dwarfism. In the past, humans have found a use for short-legged dogs and so deliberately bred from dogs with dwarfism to get more like them. A well-known example is the condition affecting the Dachshund and the Basset Hound. These breeds are chondrodystrophic – a type of dwarfism that causes those endearingly cute and ultra-short legs. Having shorter legs may have conferred an advantage on the original sporting Dachshunds, which were bred and trained to hunt badgers in their underground burrows. Shorter-legged hounds like the Basset Hound were useful to our forebears because they enabled hunt followers to keep up with the hound pack on foot.

Shortening the legs of a dog may confer some benefit to his human friends, but it also confers some disadvantages to the dog. In a working dog, these disadvantages can never be taken too far, or the dog will be unable to work and therefore of no value to his owners. In a pet dog or a dog bred for the show ring, there are no such constraints and the impact of several decades of breeding dogs with ever shorter legs is now clear. I'm afraid it isn't good news. By just *one year* of age, approximately 90 per cent of chondrodystrophic dogs are showing spinal disc degeneration that affects multiple discs. Partial or complete calcification of the disc is common. These changes can start as early as four months of age, that is just two months after you collect your perfect little Dachshund puppy from the breeder. And by 12 to 18 months of age, your puppy's discs could be completely degenerated.

Not only is their ability to run and jump impaired, the spinal problems chondrodystrophic dogs suffer from can be very painful indeed. If you have ever suffered from back pain, you'll have some idea. Universities Federation for Animal Welfare (UFAW) estimates 25 per cent of Dachshunds will suffer from intervertebral disc disease (IVDD) at some point in their lives. This includes ruptured, prolapsed, herniated and slipped discs, and other unpleasant spinal conditions that can cause paralysis and/or severe pain that is prolonged in duration. Other studies suggest that the risk for some groups or categories of Dachshund is higher still. A study published in 2013 found 38 per cent of standard Smooth-Haired Dachshunds were affected by IVDD, and a shocking 65 per cent of Miniature Smooth-Haired Dachshunds. Overall, the study showed that the smaller, Miniature Long-Backed breeds were most at risk.

As with many structural problems in dogs, if you can find a less extreme version of the breed, your dog's chances of remaining healthy may be somewhat improved, but the only way to completely avoid them is to avoid dogs with very short legs.

Twisted tails

While the wolf's tail is a straightforward extension of his spine, carried low and thickly furred, we now have dogs with tails in a range of different styles. A screw tail forms a coil on the dog's bottom and is common in Bulldogs and French Bulldogs. Screw tails frequently cause problems for the dogs that have them, and those problems may not be confined to the tail itself. The spiral shape is caused by oddly shaped spinal bones known as hemivertebrae that cause the spinal column to twist on itself. These hemivertebrae may not be confined to the tail end of the spine, and if they occur further along the dog's back they may put pressure on the spinal nerve and cause neurological problems, with symptoms such as incontinence, paralysis and severe pain. These symptoms can appear in puppyhood.

Screw tails trap faeces and dirt, and have a nasty habit of growing inwards, into the dog's body. This is known as an inverted tail and is a serious and painful problem for your dog. All screw tails easily become smelly and infected. They need daily cleaning, and if they become inverted your dog will need veterinary treatment and may need an amputation. Tightly coiled screw tails are really best avoided, and in breeds that are prone to hemivertebrae you need to ensure that the parents of your puppy have been X-rayed and shown to be clear of the condition.

Closed or pinched nostrils

If you look at a dog from the front, his nose has two openings, one either side of the mid-line, and these openings need to be a wide round O shape. If a dog has tightly pinched nostrils the openings will look more like a crescent or a crack. Pinched nostrils are a warning sign that all is not well with the dog behind them. They are associated with collapsed or obstructed airways and are common in dogs with serious breathing problems. Sadly, there are still some breeders in denial about this issue, who will tell you that pinched nostrils are normal for a breed such as a Pug or Bulldog. This is misleading because it implies that normal is the same as harmless, and this is not the case. When you are choosing a litter of puppies, make sure both parents have open nostrils. If the breeder does not own the father, ask to see a photo. Pinched nostrils can be clearly seen in a headshot, front-facing photo of the dog.

Noisy breathing and excessive panting

Some dogs make snuffling and grunting noises while they breathe. These kinds of noises are very common in Pugs, and you'll find lots of YouTube videos of Pugs snorting and snoring. These noises can sound quite cute and appealing but they are a sign of trouble. Partially obstructed airways are often the cause of such noisy breathing; they are actually a sign of discomfort in a dog that is short of oxygen. Again, this is an issue where some breeders are in denial about the health issues with their dogs. They may try to convince you that noisy breathing is OK by telling you that it is normal for the breed.

Excessive panting is not a good sign either. A dog in a cool room that is resting or moving around at a walking pace won't normally be panting. Excessive panting on the slightest movement or activity is common in dogs that have trouble cooling themselves, and the reason for both oxygenating and cooling problems is usually a side effect of breeding for a flatter face. Let's look more closely at that.

Very short muzzles

There is a very good chance that you are hoping to buy a flat-faced dog. Registration figures show that their popularity is growing at an unprecedented rate. Flat-faced (brachycephalic) dogs are created by breeding from dogs with shortened jawbones. A set-back nose may have once been a breathing advantage to a dog, such as a Bulldog, that was expected to grip or hang onto prey or livestock. Over time, however, these features have been increasingly exaggerated and this has compromised the health of several of our pedigree breeds.

Many people are surprised to find that the shape of a dog's skull is so critical to his ability to moderate his temperature. Human beings are super-efficient at cooling themselves, they do it by sweating through their skin. Dogs are

Brachycephalic breeds often have pinched nostrils.

incapable of sweating apart from through their paws, which is why they tend to rest during the heat of the day in hot climates. However, a healthy dog can maintain a reasonable body temperature in all but the most extreme temperatures and he does this by losing moisture along the surface of his mouth as he pants. As we shorten the muzzle in the domestic dog, so we reduce the area of this radiator, and the temperature of the dog begins to climb. This is why brachycephalic dogs must not be exercised in warm weather. They suffer easily from heatstroke, which can be fatal. The shorter the muzzle, the worse the problem.

There is another, serious problem with brachycephaly, and that is the way it interferes with the dog's ability to oxygenate himself. When we breed dogs with short facial bones, the soft tissues that surround those jawbones are not reduced proportionately. This leaves an excess of skin on the outside, and an excess of tissue on the inside of the dog's mouth. The excess skin on the outside forms folds around the dog's nose, trapping dirt, and sometimes rubbing against the surface of his eyes, causing intense pain and infection. On the inside, the excess tissue can block the dog's airway, causing obstructed breathing, fainting and even death.

Brachycephalic skulls crowd other organs too. Insufficient space for brain tissue and overly shallow eye sockets are not good news for dogs born with flatter faces than nature intended, and the short jawbones of the brachycephalic dog still have to contain the same number of teeth found in any other breed. There isn't room for them, so the teeth will be crowded and may require extensive dental work to prevent pain and repeated infections.

A recent important study by the UFAW on the impact of facial structure on canine health showed respiratory problems in dogs increase in direct proportion to the decrease in muzzle length relative to the rest of the skull. Yet we are breeding dogs with ever flatter faces, and there are currently no regulations concerning the length of muzzle a dog should have before being allowed to produce puppies.

There is no doubt that people find flat-faced dogs very appealing to look at. And many people buy them because they are also looking for a low-energy dog. The sad truth is that flat-faced dogs cannot cool themselves or breathe easily, so they don't run about much. Not because they lack enthusiasm, but in order to stay alive. They may find it difficult to sleep when they lie down and will try to fall asleep sitting up or with their head propped against something. They are liable to fainting, and serious breathing problems where the airway becomes obstructed. Surgical repairs to the airway are sometimes possible, but will cost you a small mortgage. Not to mention the heartache that comes with watching a dog struggle to breathe on a daily basis, or cope with major surgery. In some breeds, Pugs and Bulldogs for example, brachycephaly is obvious and severe. Some milder cases of brachycephaly are harder to spot, but big prominent doe eyes are an indication of the problems ahead.

Bulging eyes

Bulging eyes are often seen in flat-faced or very small dogs like the Chihuahua. They are a sign that the dog's skull is not quite big enough for what needs to fit inside. Compression of the brain caused by too small a skull is what gives our beautiful Cavalier King Charles Spaniel his endearing doe-eyed expression, but it is also what has crippled the breed with the devastating neurological condition called syringomyelia.

Not only are bulging eyes a symptom of insufficient space in the skull, the eyes themselves are vulnerable to injury. In a healthy dog the eyes are recessed into the skull to give them some bony protection from knocks and scratches. If the eyes project further than they should from the safety of the skull they become vulnerable to injury. More importantly, if the eyes bulge too much, the eyelids don't meet in the centre of the eye when the dog sleeps or blinks. This causes corneal problems and severe distress to the dog. Last but not least, bulging eyes have a propensity to literally pop right out of their sockets. A horrible experience for the dog, and anyone present.

Skinfolds

We may not like wrinkles on ourselves, but we just love them on our dogs. Loose skin and skinfolds are very appealing. Facial folds can give expression to a dog's face – puppies often look more cuddly than adult dogs partly because they have not quite 'grown into their skin'. We have now bred deep skinfolds into some of our domestic dog breeds. And in the last 50 or 60 years, this wrinkling of the skin has been greatly exaggerated by selective breeding. Breeds like the Shar Pei and the Neapolitan Mastiff are now deeply wrinkled. Sounds pretty harmless, right? Unfortunately, as is often the case with exaggerations in structure, there are disadvantages to the dog and, as a consequence, to the dog's family. Let's have a closer look at why that is.

If a dog's skin is too deeply wrinkled, dirt and debris gets trapped in the folds. Shaking, in a dog with normal skin, is a great way to free fur from debris and liquid, but in a dog with deep skinfolds it is less effective. The dog cannot keep itself clean and the creases in the skin then become infected. This is why the owners of dogs with skinfolds, whether it is just around the nose (as in some flat-faced dogs) or around the tail (screw-tailed dogs) or over much more of the body, must be rigorous about cleaning in between the skinfolds on a daily basis. Even with good care, skin infections are common in wrinkled dogs. Loose skin, a prerequisite for wrinkling, also causes painful eye problems.

If you look at a dog like the Neapolitan Mastiff you will see that the enormous weight of excess skin is unable to withstand the force of gravity. The skin of the face sags downwards, exposing the delicate mucous membranes below the eye. This predisposes the dog to repeated painful infections. Sadly, this occurs in many dogs that have been bred with too much skin, especially those we have come to associate with droopy lower eyes – like the Bloodhound and the Basset Hound.

In some cases, severe loose skin and wrinkling will require surgical intervention to make the dog comfortable again. Many vets are also concerned at the increase in wrinkling and loose skin they are seeing in breeds that were not previously associated with this condition. Great Danes, for example, can now be found with areas of sore exposed mucous membrane beneath each eye, and long hanging jowls. Even some of our Gundog breeds have been mildly affected in this way, with drooping lower eyelids and jowls creeping into some of our Spaniel breeds.

If a breed of dog that is subject to wrinkling really appeals to you, then you need to try and find the most moderate type in order to reduce some of these problems. Sadly, the only way to avoid them completely is to avoid choosing a breed of dog with very wrinkly or saggy skin.

Banana backs

You'll notice dogs in the show ring are often 'stacked', or stood with their back feet further back than is natural, in order to accentuate the slope of the dog's topline, something that some show breeders find attractive. From a health point of view, your dog's back needs to be fairly level, at least when he is standing naturally. A slight slope from shoulders to rump (or occasionally the other way) may not be a problem, but anything more can cause problems for the dog. This is because the spine does not exist in isolation. It connects with the legs at the hips and shoulders and the angles at which all these joints fit together is crucial to the dog's health. It's about mechanics. And we interfere with those mechanics at the dog's peril.

Most German Shepherd dog breeders who exhibit their dogs in the ring favour a sloping topline, and this feature has become increasingly exaggerated over the past few years. Many have actually bred into their dogs a curve or banana shape to the spine that is quite distinctive. This gives a dog a steeply sloping topline even when it isn't stacked, and changes the dog's gait through greatly increased angulation of the hind legs. Rear-leg angulation is seen as a positive thing by GSD breeders because it increases stride length, which generates more efficient movement. However, like most aspects of body structure, more is not necessarily better. Veterinary canine performance expert Christine Zink talks about why a balance is important when it comes to angulation in her article 'Form Follows Function – A New Perspective on an Old Adage'.

Zink explains that when you increase angulation too much, the back end of the dog becomes unstable. We now see GSDs in the show ring with their back legs wobbling as they run. Another extreme and severe side effect of this bowing of the spine is that the GSD is forced to run on his hocks. Dogs are what we call digitigrade animals, which simply means they run on their toes. In a healthy dog the hock or equivalent of our heel is raised high in the air and never comes into contact with the ground. Some GSDs have such extreme angulation that they are forced into a plantigrade action where the whole foot, including the hock, strikes the ground just as it does in humans.

The Kennel Club are trying to address this problem in show lines of GSDs and have put the GSD into category 3 (the highest category) of their Breed Watch scheme. We'll be talking more about the Breed Watch scheme and how it can help you choose your puppy in part three, chapter four.

Giant dogs like this handsome Wolfhound have shorter lifespans.

Extremes of size

A lot of people group dogs by size when considering a breed. This is not such a bad idea as your home environment may well influence the size of the dog you decide to share your life with. However, you may be interested to know that extremes of size can also influence the health of your dog. In nature, larger species of animal tend to outlive the tiny ones. Elephants outlive mice, and your pony will probably outlive your rabbit, for example. So you might expect big dogs to outlive tiny ones. But dogs, despite their different appearance, are a single species, and within a species, extremes of size are often disadvantageous. This is as true for dogs as for people, where gigantism is also associated with a shorter lifespan. The hard fact is: giant dogs don't live as long as smaller dogs. And we are not talking months here, we are talking years. Your Dogue de Bordeaux may be lucky to make it to five-and-a-half years old, while your neighbour's Miniature Poodle could well be her constant companion for the next 15 years. Many people purchasing a giant breed puppy are not aware of this.

If you are undaunted by their short lifespan, you still need to consider the practicalities of looking after one of our beautiful giant breeds. Your Irish Wolfhound may only last six years or so, but he'll eat his way through a fair proportion of your wages each week. Veterinary care, insurance, boarding kennel fees, etc., all cost more for a giant dog than for his smaller cousins. Most dogs take up to two years to become adult, giant dogs can take even longer. To lose a dog just two or three years later seems a very high price to pay for owning a really big dog.

Normal for the breed

The 'breed standard' for any given breed is a set of criteria governing the appearance and temperament of that breed. Breed standards were usually drawn up by breed clubs, most of which were formed decades ago, and these standards are overseen by the Kennel Club and displayed on their website. One thing that puppy buyers will routinely hear when they ask questions about the structure of a particular dog is that it is 'normal for the breed'. Pugs are supposed to have flat faces, Dachshunds are supposed to have short legs, it says so in the breed standard. And that may well be true. Because in the UK and US right now, and in other countries too, it is perfectly legal to have breed standards for one breed of dog which specify characteristics that would be considered a serious disability in another breed.

Breed standards are created by people and can be changed and updated, though major changes are not common. Many of those concerned with dog welfare would like to see some sweeping changes made to breed standards. One of the most basic requirements for a happy life for any dog is a well-structured, fully functioning body. Most people would agree that every dog should have the ability to breathe easily, maintain a normal body temperature, and to run, jump and swim. It doesn't seem reasonable that these benefits should be available to some breeds and denied others.

The problems you can't see

One last consideration before we leave the topic of structure is your dog's ability to get along with other dogs. Dogs communicate with one another via body language. They signal with tail position and posture, invite play using 'play bows' and play with one another by chasing and allowing themselves to be chased. If their structure is altered from the primitive wolf blueprint, some dogs may find it difficult to 'talk' to other dogs. In some cases, this can be quite a handicap for the dog concerned.

SUMMARY

We have looked in this chapter at problems you can see with your own eyes. These are issues you can easily avoid, simply by avoiding breeds, or in some cases lines of 'related' dogs, that carry them. The problems you cannot see are perhaps more of a challenge. Problems that lurk inside dogs, often skipping generations and reappearing where least expected. Fortunately, there are ways to reduce the risk of these problems too. So let's move on to Chapter 5 and find out what they are.

5
Healthy Genes

At one time, the main threat to the health of most puppies came from infectious diseases and accidents. In many parts of the world today, this is no longer true. Widespread vaccination campaigns during the late twentieth century dramatically decreased the chances of a dog dying before his first birthday. For many modern dogs illnesses caused by structural defects and inherited diseases pose a far greater threat to happiness and longevity than the risk of infection. In the last chapter we looked in detail at how best you can avoid your new puppy suffering from one of the disabilities that have been unwittingly bioengineered into a number of our popular dog breeds today. In this chapter we are going to look at the diseases that lurk beneath the surface, the diseases that are passed down from one generation to the next.

Your dog's genes will influence his future health.

How genes work to build a dog

Every puppy is born with thousands of genes, which create the blueprint for the dog he will become. These genes are stored on long strands of DNA, and a copy of these strands lies in the nucleus of every single cell in your puppy's body. This genetic information or gene store is a kind of 'control room' that tells your puppy how to grow and behave. Working together with the effects of his environment, it controls every aspect of your puppy's development.

Genes control the problems we looked at in the last chapter and many of your dog's attributes too. While environmental factors can sometimes influence the final outcome, genes often determine potential, such as how big your puppy will grow or how fast he will be able to run, as well as specifics, such as appearance – what colour his coat or eyes will be. Though environment is a powerful influence on temperament, genes also control, to some extent, how friendly or shy your puppy will be. Genes are also responsible for a range of inherited diseases. Diseases which you do not want your puppy to suffer from, and which are difficult to eradicate without causing *more* diseases in the process. I'll explain that in a moment.

How genes cause diseases

Genes that cause diseases are basically a faulty or altered copy of a gene that should be responsible for some aspect of your dog's normal development. If a gene is faulty, it may interfere with that normal development. Sometimes genes are responsible for the production of important chemicals or hormones in your dog's body. When a dog inherits the faulty gene he may be unable to produce those chemicals or hormones and so develops a disease which may make him very sick or even kill him. Some genes change the structure of your dog, some alter the way nerves or muscles work, or the way an organ interacts with another organ. The body is such an incredibly complex mix of structures and processes, all working in perfect harmony in the healthy animal, it is perhaps amazing that we see as few diseases as we do.

If we can identify the individual faulty gene that causes a disease, there is often a good chance that we can test for it. We now have DNA tests for a number of diseases that puppies can inherit from their parents. The most common tests you'll come across as you search for a puppy are for autosomal recessive diseases. It helps to understand how these work and what the results mean.

Autosomal recessive diseases

In very simple terms, genes for each attribute your dog possesses come together in pairs; your puppy inherits two genes for each attribute, one from each of his parents. There are thousands of these pairs of genes in every dog, each pair responsible for some specific aspect of your dog's development. Genes can be one of two types, dominant or recessive. The potential for recessive disease occurs when a recessive gene is faulty. But this disease potential is only realised if the dog inherits two copies of the faulty gene, one from each parent. This is because dominant genes overpower recessive genes and render them harmless. The dominant gene acts effectively as a switch, turning off the recessive gene, and preventing it from causing mischief. In this way faulty recessive genes can be passed down through the generations, paired with dominant genes, their potential for harm hidden away until two of them come together.

Each puppy can inherit one of three possible combinations of genes:

1. **Dominant + Dominant**
2. **Dominant + Recessive**
3. **Recessive + Recessive**

If we change this diagram to reflect the impact of these genes, it looks like this:

1. **Normal + Normal = clear/unaffected (healthy dog)**
2. **Normal + Faulty = carrier (healthy dog)**
3. **Faulty + Faulty = affected (diseased dog)**

Dog 1 – clear

Dog 1 is known as clear or unaffected. He can never get sick from this disease and he can never pass it on.

Dog 2 – carrier

Dog 2 can never get sick because his normal gene switches off the faulty one so he makes a perfectly good family pet. However, he must be bred from with great caution because he has the potential to pass the faulty gene on to his puppies. He is known as a carrier. Interestingly, dog 2 can be bred from provided he is mated to dog 1, but some of his puppies will be carriers and must also be bred from with caution. To avoid affected puppies, a carrier must never be mated with another carrier, or with an affected dog.

Dog 3 – affected

Remember that dominant genes 'switch off' the recessive genes, so only dog 3 will become sick. Dogs that DNA test for recessive + recessive are called affected. At some point he will develop the condition that is coded into the faulty gene. Many inherited diseases are passed on in this way, on a recessive gene.

🐾 SUMMARY

- Rare recessive genes can stay hidden for generations. There are thousands, if not millions, of potentially harmful recessive genes hidden in the wider dog population (just as in our human population) that never cause a problem because they are so rare, they hardly ever arise together in the same individual.
- So why is it that new diseases seem to be appearing more frequently now? Let's have a look.

What defines genetic health?

In a genetically varied population where no one is very closely related, genetic diseases are the exception. Nasty genes are rare, and in a healthy population they remain rare. But occasionally a small population of animals becomes isolated from others of the same species. The individuals in the group are then paired up with others that share some of the same genetic material, a process we refer to as inbreeding. When this happens, the risk of two disease-bearing genes getting together begins to rise.

Achieving a good level of genetic health in any population of animals is about reducing the risk of those nasty recessive genes getting together in a matching pair. And there are two keys to this process:

- **Maintaining genetic variety in a population**
- **Maintaining a large enough population.**

Low genetic variety increases the chances of two identical genes getting together, and small populations increase the level of inbreeding, which also increases the chances of two bad genes meeting up.

Studies made of 'island populations' of animals show that there are several symptoms of poor genetic health in isolated groups. In addition to increasing levels of disease and disability, fertility levels fall and individuals are less likely to become pregnant. Litter sizes diminish and birth weights decline. It isn't always possible to identify a single gene or combination of genes that cause these problems in island populations, but the signs of poor genetic health, including rising levels of disease, are clearly associated with rising levels of inbreeding.

The reason this may affect you and your puppy is because every dog breed registered with the Kennel Club today is, in effect, an island population. The breed registers are closed and outcrossing between one breed and another is prohibited. Several other factors have accelerated genetic problems in our pedigree dog breeds. One is the overuse of popular sires. Another is the culture of line breeding, so beloved of the dog breeding community. Line breeding is not a subtly different type of inbreeding, it is simply another word for the same practice of mating closely related dogs to one another.

Until recently, the dog breeding community's strategy for dealing with inherited diseases in dogs has been to promote and encourage the widespread uptake of health screening. That sounds like a good idea, right?

Why not just test all dogs for diseases?

To understand why health screening isn't the long-term answer to genetic problems in dogs we need to quickly examine the root cause of poor genetic health in closed or island populations. In any living species, genes, common genes and rare genes alike are constantly being lost from a population. This happens because some members of any population will never get to breed and pass their genes on. In a healthy population this doesn't matter, because new genes are being brought into the community at regular intervals, as newcomers arrive and join. In an island population this cannot happen. No new genes are coming in, so the total number of genes within the population becomes inexorably smaller. The smaller the gene pool, the greater the chances of bad

Every pedigree dog breed registered today is, in effect, an island population.

genes bumping up against one another. In very small populations this process is exacerbated and accelerated. The end result is the end of the population. And the smaller the population, the sooner the end will arrive.

Health testing does not address the cause of the problem, indeed it can actually make the problem worse. This is because eliminating animals from breeding removes yet *more* genes from the already diminishing gene pool. (As does a widespread policy of neutering our pets.)

The extent of this problem has been repeatedly highlighted by populations geneticists for some time now, and the information does appear to be filtering down to some dog breeders. The faith that dog breeders have placed in health testing is beginning to waver a little. Breeders are beginning to address the underlying cause of genetic poor health, which is of course inbreeding.

The Kennel Club have begun helping breeders to understand and calculate how inbred their dogs are, and to provide a means of calculating the level of inbreeding that would occur in any litter between two dogs, before the mating even takes place. It is done with a calculation called the coefficient of inbreeding (COI). You need to know a little about this coefficient before you buy a puppy.

Coefficient of inbreeding

The coefficient of inbreeding is the probability that a dog will inherit two copies of the identical gene from an ancestor that occurs on both sides of his family tree. The purpose of calculating the COI of any dog is to establish how likely it is that his ancestors are closely related. The higher the COI, the more closely related the dog's ancestors and therefore the more likely it is that his parents will be genetically similar too. If two puppies from the same litter were mated to each other, for example, they would be statistically likely to share 25 per cent of their genetic information – that would be expressed as a COI of 25 per cent – not a desirable situation and one that greatly increases the chances of producing sick puppies through the pairing of faulty recessive genes. A mother-to-son mating, or father-to-daughter mating would be the same, a COI of 25 per cent. Obviously this too would create a high risk of two harmful recessive genes being paired together. If we mate a grandfather to granddaughter, we get a COI of 12.5 per cent and first cousins gives us 6.25 per cent.

Our understanding of how coefficients of inbreeding affect the genetic health of a breed is still growing. We know that it isn't just a question of increasing the risk of new diseases appearing in a breed, but that there are wider implications to inbreeding. The adverse effects of inbreeding become evident when the COI of a mating exceeds 5 per cent. By 10 per cent the adverse effect becomes significant. The Institute of Canine Biology states that these effects include a loss of vitality in offspring and an increase in recessive mutations. A German study of inbreeding in Dachshunds showed that litter size decreased, and the percentage of puppies born dead increased, with increasing coefficients of inbreeding. As populations become smaller, rates of inbreeding rise, causing smaller populations. A 10 per cent coefficient of inbreeding is considered by biologists to be the threshold for triggering this negative spiral known as the 'extinction vortex'. Yet it is not unusual for the average coefficient of inbreeding in a pedigree breed of dog to exceed this figure.

How you can choose a puppy with healthy genes

Inbreeding has caused a range of common diseases in our pedigree breeds, and will cause new diseases in the future. While health testing is not a long-term solution for the survival of our pedigree breeds, it is still important for you and your puppy. To give your puppy the best chance of avoiding known diseases, you should ensure that all the relevant health tests have been carried out on his parents. Each Breed Review in Part Two details the tests needed, and Part Three gives information on where to look for breeds not listed in this book.

To reduce the risk of an as-yet-unknown disease appearing in your puppy, and to help improve the genetic health of your chosen breed, you should do your best to ensure that your puppy has as low a coefficient of inbreeding as possible. You'll need to have realistic expectations though. Inbreeding (line breeding) has been hugely popular with pedigree dog breeders for decades, primarily because it works very well to fix desirable characteristics including physical attributes and behavioural traits. If you are choosing a pedigree puppy, then you will need to accept a certain level of inbreeding in his ancestors. Now that the potential for irretrievable harm to our pedigree breeds is understood, modern dog breeders should no longer be line breeding, but this is a relatively new turn of events and not all breeders are up to date so you need to take responsibility yourself for ensuring that your puppy does not come from two closely related parents.

You can find out the coefficient of inbreeding in the health section of each breed review, and the COI for all breeds are listed on the KC website. Your aim should be to deliberately select a breeder who has made a determined effort to ensure a low COI (under 5 per cent) for your puppy. You can also use the Kennel Club's COI calculator to work out the coefficient of inbreeding of any litter you intend to visit. We'll come back to this when we look at finding a litter in Part Three.

Where does this leave pedigree dogs?

You may have concluded from reading all this that pedigree dogs are all doomed and that you would be better off buying a crossbred puppy or mongrel. But life is rarely that straightforward. A puppy is not just a product of his structure and his genes. He is also a product of his environment, of the way he has been raised. For the first eight weeks of his life, your puppy was in the care of another human being, and their actions during that time play an important role in the dog he will become. This means that when we purchase a puppy, we need to consider where puppies come from, where they are being bought and sold, in addition to the health issues we have already discussed.

In the next chapter we'll compare pedigree puppies with crossbred and mongrel puppies. We'll talk about health and temperament, but also about the influence of the puppy's origins on the way he is likely to be raised.

6
Pedigree or Mongrel?

In this chapter we are going to look at the pedigree versus mixed-breed dog debate, and help you to decide which is for you. We have spent some time now looking at what makes a healthy dog, in terms of both the way a dog is structured and the genetic information locked away in his DNA. On the basis of what we have learned, it would be easy to assume that pedigree dogs are a disaster, and that you would be better off rushing out to buy the first

Some people prefer cross-bred dogs to pedigrees.

mongrel you come across than considering a purebred pedigree dog. But life isn't quite that simple.

I'll declare myself at this point and make it clear that I own four pedigree purebred dogs. What is more, my next puppy will probably be a pedigree dog too. That may seem confusing, but I hope that by the end of this chapter, my reasons will be clear.

What we mean by pedigree

Pedigree dogs are not a modern invention. In fact, there were pedigree dogs long before any of the world's kennel clubs were formed. If we take the word literally, a pedigree is simply an ancestral or genealogical record. People breeding dogs for a particular role, whether it be Sheepdogs for herding, Sled dogs for hauling, or Hounds for hunting, often kept detailed records. They would know the parents, grandparents and great-grandparents of each puppy born, how many puppies were born in each litter, their weights and much more was recorded. The Beaufort Hunt, for example, has pedigree records dating right back to the mid-eighteenth century. These stud books were important documents tracing the ancestry of each line back over many years. So if a pedigree is simply a record of ancestry, what is different about the breeds that most of us think of as pedigree dogs? The answer lies not in the word pedigree, but in the word purebred.

A badge of quality?

All the dogs on the Kennel Club breed registers are purebred. When I was a child, in the 1960s, for most people pedigree registration and ownership of a purebred dog were considered a badge of quality. By purebred, of course, we mean puppies that arise from a mating between two dogs on the same breed register. The purebred dog was considered to be a superior animal to his mixed-breed cousins. That isn't to say there were no concerns about pedigree dogs and the way they were bred but, in general, the public perception of a pedigree dog and of pedigree dog breeders was a positive one. Pedigree dog breeders were accorded some status, and were often respected members of their local community.

This position has been severely rocked in the last decade, and the public perception of breeders has suffered. While there was already concern over the health of our purebred breeds, especially among veterinarians, that concern was accelerated in 2008 when film producer and journalist Jemima Harrison released her controversial and thought-provoking film *Pedigree Dogs Exposed*.

A fall from grace

Pedigree Dogs Exposed shook the dog world to its roots. It altered, perhaps forever, the public perception of pedigree dogs and those closely involved with them. The film exposed the structural problems present in many breeds and highlighted how some breeders were pursuing ever more exaggerated versions of their breed standards. It called into question the age-old practice of inbreeding (line breeding) and drew attention to some of the unpleasant diseases now appearing in our purebred dogs. The shocking footage of dogs with painful and distressing health conditions had a profound effect on the public conscience to an extent that no previous campaigner for canine welfare had ever been able to achieve.

Perhaps the most controversial aspect of the film was that it questioned the morality and wisdom of breeding dogs within closed gene pools. Questioning the superiority of the purebred dogs was an alien concept to many of us who were still firmly in the 'pedigree is best' camp. Dog breeders everywhere were exposed to a backlash from the general public and a widespread fall in status, no matter what breed of dog they specialised in. Many members of the dog-breeding community saw the film as a direct and very personal attack on their way of life. They also saw it as a threat to their position as responsible guardians of our dogs' health and welfare. It was an uncomfortable time for the Kennel Club and it is probably fair to say that their prestige has never quite regained its previous status.

The film also set a lot of people wondering. 'Should I buy a pedigree dog, or would I be better off with a mixed breed?' Registrations of purebred dogs fell in the subsequent years, and a roller coaster of changes has been put into place by the Kennel Club to address concerns about the health and long-term survival of many of our pedigree breeds.

In addition to the banning of brother/sister, father/daughter, and mother/son matings, the Kennel Club has introduced a Breed Watch scheme aimed at show judges. The scheme highlights points of concern about exaggerations of conformation in individual breeds in an attempt to improve their structure. The Kennel Club has also introduced the Mate Select programme, which helps breeders make better breeding choices and helps puppy buyers choose puppies from litters with more genetic diversity. Though some would like to see the Kennel Club go much further, these are important steps that make a start in improving the health of our pedigree breeds.

We have talked quite a bit about the problems with pedigree dogs, and I want to now look at the other side of the coin. Let's talk about some of the benefits of owning a purebred puppy.

A predictable appearance

While generations of inbreeding have created problems for our dogs, that inbreeding was originally carried out for a reason. The benefits of inbreeding include some of the qualities we see in our pedigree breeds today. The first and clearest benefit of buying a pedigree puppy is that you know exactly what your puppy will look like when he grows up. A purebred pedigree gives you consistency and predictability of appearance. If you buy a Golden Retriever you know you are going to get a largish dog with floppy ears and a medium-length coat that will require a bit of grooming. You know he will be a golden yellow colour and, with the appropriate care and training, will probably be a good-tempered and obedient family dog.

If you breed a Labrador to a Labrador, the puppies will all look like Labradors. No one questions this. The same is not true, for example, of first crosses. If you breed two identical Labradoodles together you won't get more identical Labradoodles, you will get much more variety, particularly in coat length, texture and colour, some of which will reflect the different breed grandparents of the puppies. In other words, crossbreeds when mated together do not breed true to type; pedigree dogs do. This element of predictability is very reassuring to most of us. The ability to produce puppies with a predictable appearance, generation after generation, is one of the benefits of buying purebred puppies today.

Instincts and capabilities

If you want a dog with a particular ability, or natural instinct, a purebred puppy will help you achieve that. I know when I buy a purebred Cocker puppy from working lines, for example, that my dog will probably have a strong hunting instinct, and enthusiasm for fetching stuff! As a trainer of Gundogs this is important to me. Just as a shepherd needs a Sheepdog that at least has a passing interest in herding sheep.

But this goes further than the instincts required for dogs destined for service roles or a job of work. We also get some predictability in purebred puppies in terms of temperament. We discussed this in Chapter 3, and it is an important point to consider. Buying a Golden Retriever puppy won't guarantee you a friendly, easy-going dog, but it certainly tips the odds in your favour.

Of course, inbreeding is not the only way to create and fix great qualities in a breed, and we now know of the potential for harm. But when pedigree dogs were first established, over a hundred years ago, it was the only way that was understood, and it produced the results we enjoy today: dogs that give birth to puppies with a predictable appearance, a predictable temperament and predictable abilities.

Opportunities for recreation and sport

Knowing your dog is likely to have certain skills is certainly an advantage, but if you want to take those skills further and compete with your dog, you may find that a pedigree, and the paper trail that goes with it, is a basic requirement. In most countries, rightly or wrongly, there are a number of activities that are restricted to purebred pedigree dogs, and this is because these activities are controlled by that country's kennel club. They include all field trials and working tests for Gundogs, and entry into dog shows. That may not matter to you right now, but I have come across a number of people over the years that have surprised themselves with their own success in training a young crossbred Gundog, and have been deeply disappointed to discover that they are excluded from competition. The same exclusion rule applies to dogs that are allegedly purebred but without papers.

Standards in dog breeding and puppy care

There is another important consideration when it comes to buying a puppy, and that is the question of quality control in the whole dog-breeding process. This includes not only questions about how a puppy is constructed and how the parents are selected, but also how the pregnant bitch is cared for, how the puppies are raised and what kind of after-sales support is provided. What happens to your puppy in the first eight weeks of his life can strongly influence how he develops, both physically and mentally. A healthy happy puppy will have had good nourishment, both while growing inside his mother and afterwards. He will also have made good progress towards becoming sociable and confident. There are a number of factors that influence a breeder's ability to provide that kind of care and those factors include knowledge, experience, commitment and time.

Choosing a pedigree puppy does not guarantee you high standards in puppy care, but it can be argued that dog breeders with high standards are more likely to be found among the pedigree dog breeding community. There is little doubt that a breeder who has raised numerous litters and has the added motivation of a reputation to maintain is likely to bring all these factors and more into play. Many breeders of pedigree dogs exhibit their dogs in the show ring or are enthusiastic competitors in some kind of dog sport, field trials or working trials, for example. A pedigree dog breeder who is successful in the show ring or field will have built up a reputation and some 'status' within the dog world. Such a person may well have dedicated their life to breeding dogs and their reputation is very important to them. Many breeders work hard at maintaining that reputation and that includes keeping to high standards of animal husbandry. They behave in a manner that they believe is in keeping with responsible breeding. This often includes outstanding after-sales support.

After-sales support

A dedicated and knowledgeable breeder is also likely to provide aftercare for their puppy buyers, offering welcome advice and support to new puppy owners long after they have adopted their puppies. Not only is this advice willingly given, usually for the lifetime of the dog, it is often high-quality advice as the experienced breeder is likely to have whelped multiple litters and successfully raised multiple dogs. A responsible breeder will usually take back a puppy they have bred at any time, should the new owner find himself unable to keep it. It is hard to put a price on this kind of support, but for many new puppy owners it is invaluable.

Again, choosing a pedigree breeder does not guarantee you high standards of after-sales care, but it is possible they are more likely to be found among the pedigree dog-breeding community.

It is clear then that there are benefits to buying a pedigree puppy. The question we now need to ask is: how do the advantages and disadvantages of buying a mixed-breed dog match up with the advantages and disadvantages of buying a pedigree puppy?

To try and figure this out we need to ask if mongrels are intrinsically healthier than pedigree dogs, and whether they are more or less likely to be raised as responsibly as their well-bred cousins.

Are mixed-breed dogs healthier?

A mongrel is a dog of unknown or mixed parentage. Within the broad definition of 'mongrel' or mixed-breed dog are numerous types of dog, some of which you will recognise and all of which are often regarded as 'inferior' animals by those who breed and exhibit purebred dogs. When two pedigree dogs from different breeds are deliberately mated together the outcome is usually referred to as a crossbreed. One particular type of crossbreed that has rapidly grown in popularity in the last ten years is a range of Poodle crosses, or Doodles. We'll be looking more closely at Doodles in Part Two.

We know that mixed-breed dogs have more genetic variety than pedigree dogs. The coefficient of inbreeding is going to be much lower, and therefore the risk of inherited disorders should be less. This seems to be borne out by the research. A study by A.R. Michell of 3,000 British dogs in 1999 showed that mongrels lived longer than most purebreds and were only outlived by Jack Russell Terriers, Miniature Poodles and Whippets. A more recent study published in 2013 looked at the longevity and mortality of dogs owned in the UK. Electronic patient records were collected from veterinary practices in south-east and central England and the deaths of over 5,000 dogs were analysed. It was discovered that crossbred dogs lived 1.2 years longer than purebred dogs. That is quite a significant life extension. Further research by insurers backs up this evidence. This work is ongoing and more data is needed, but again only two breeds – the Border Collie and the English Springer – outlived mixed breeds. Longevity is undeniably related to health so these figures should not be ignored or discounted.

What about designer dogs?

'Designer dogs' is a term coined for increasingly popular first crosses between some of our pedigree dogs. These breeds are more genetically diverse than purebred dogs but it does not mean they will be free from problems. Some pedigree breeds share the same inherited disorders, and the crossbred puppy from them will be susceptible to that disorder too. Purchasing a Labradoodle, for example, won't help you avoid hip dysplasia in your pet or progressive retinal atrophy (PRA). You still need to test for these things.

In some cases, designer dogs are a great improvement health-wise on at least one of the parent breeds. This is particularly the case where one of the parents has been bred with a structural defect, such as brachycephaly.

Brachycephalic dogs are the flat-faced breeds, which are prone to serious respiratory problems, and purchasing a purebred brachycephalic puppy is a risky business. Brachycephaly is such a serious disability that crossing a brachycephalic dog such as a Pug with a dog that has a muzzle is likely to produce healthier puppies than those from two brachycephalic parents. In other words, you would probably be better off with a Puggle (a Beagle crossed with a Pug) than with a Pug, though the mix may not be an improvement from the Beagle's point of view.

Many of our popular crossbreeds have a Poodle parent like this one.

The arguments against designer dogs can be quite emotive, but it is probably reasonable to say that some designer dog breeders are just interested in cashing in on the sudden popularity and demand for a new trend. This can push prices up way beyond what people would normally expect to pay for a purebred puppy, and may attract some breeders who are not particularly interested in dog welfare. However, the same is also true of some breeders producing pedigree puppies from fashionable or popular breeds.

The arguments against mixed-breed puppies

One of the problems with mixed-breed dogs is predicting temperament and other characteristics. If I cross a Labrador with a Border Collie, for example, there is no guarantee I'll get a dog that loves both herding and retrieving. I could end up with a dog that loves neither. And if I buy a mixed-breed puppy whose father is out of the picture, I won't really have any idea what my dog might look or behave like once he is fully grown. As I am not a fan of dog grooming, I'd have to hope he wasn't an Afghan Hound.

One of the arguments pedigree dog breeders use to oppose the sale or purchase of mongrels is that mongrels are not health tested. The opposing argument is that the genetic diversity is improved for most mongrels to the extent that the risks from inherited disease are greatly reduced. Some 'designer dog' breeders are now testing their breeding stock for the relevant health disorders, and it is also worth pointing out that pure breeding is no guarantee of health tests either. According to a study published in 2010, 50 to 60 per cent of Labrador Retrievers used for breeding have been hip scored. That means 40 to 50 per cent of purebred pedigree Labrador puppies come from parents that have *not* been health tested, despite hip dysplasia being a horrible and potentially crippling condition that is common in the breed.

We have looked at the importance of an experienced and knowledgeable person being involved in the care and welfare of your puppy in those important early weeks. It is often argued that such care is less likely to be forthcoming from a breeder of designer dogs, or from a puppy that is the result of an accidental mating. If you buy a crossbred puppy from the nice young couple down the road whose bitch got pregnant by mistake, are they going to be able to help you when you phone them in a panic because your puppy has stopped eating or won't stop biting your toddler? Can you be sure that the puppy wasn't shut away in a back room for days on end because they both work or are wrapped up in their own kids? And will they take the puppy back and look after it if your daughter develops an allergy to the dog or your husband moves out and you have to move into a 'no pets' flat? The chances are, with the best will in the world, the young couple in question won't be equipped to help you.

Of course there are many exceptions. Some mixed-breed puppies are raised with absolute dedication and care. And, to be fair, many people don't need or want the kind of after care or support an experienced breeder can offer. When considering a mixed breed, you will need to judge each case on its own merits. My personal feeling is that if you are lucky enough to find a home-bred designer dog, with the relevant health tests in place, or a well-cared for mongrel brought up in the family kitchen surrounded by children and the comings and goings of family life, and you feel confident enough to go ahead, then don't discount these dogs from your search.

A summary of pros and cons

There are clearly potential benefits to buying both pedigree and mixed-breed puppies.

With a pedigree puppy you get a predictable outcome with regard to the typical characteristics of each breed. In many cases (not all) you also get access to an experienced, knowledgeable breeder using health-tested dogs and offering high-quality care to your puppy. There are some pedigree breeds which are simply not suitable pets for anyone hoping for a dog with a long and healthy life ahead of him, but there is certainly no need to discount all pedigree dogs out of hand.

With mixed-breed puppies we see greater longevity than in most pedigree breeds, and this is likely to be a reflection of an improvement in overall health. Arguably, with a mixed-breed puppy, you will be unlikely to be able to predict his adult-dog structure or temperament. You are also less likely to have access to an experienced and knowledgeable breeder. And if health tests are necessary, as they are in some of our designer breeds, you may be less likely to have access to those.

There are commercial breeders producing both popular pedigree and mixed-breed puppies so choosing pedigree over mongrel, or vice versa, will not protect you from puppy farmers. I'll explain in Part Three how to avoid those.

The overall message here is that we need to look at any litter of puppies on a case-by-case basis, not ruling anything out, but being aware of the pitfalls before visiting a litter from any source. Whether or not a pedigree breed is right for you and your family will depend partly on the kind of dog you are attracted to. We can't just lump pedigree dogs together, nor for that matter can we assume that all mixed-breed dogs share the same attributes. The potential for a long and happy life is something that varies from breed to breed, and even from dog to dog.

So to help make that decision, we'll need to focus more closely on the type of dog you have in mind. Let's move on now and explore the world of pedigree dogs a little further. We'll start by getting to grips with the seven different groups of dog that are available to you.

7

The Seven Dog Groups

The next few chapters are all about narrowing down your choice. The Kennel Club (KC) have divided the world of dogs into seven different groups. Pedigree dogs all belong to one of these groups and the information about them is relevant to many crossbred puppies. If you are not sure what type of dog you want to bring into your life, understanding a little about the origins and characteristics of each group may help. In this chapter, we'll be looking briefly at each of the groups in order of popularity.

It is interesting to compare how the balance of popularity between the different groups has changed over the last few years. I have put the Kennel Club group registration figures (rounded up to the nearest thousand) into the table below. Overall, dog registration figures have fallen over the last decade, by around 19 per cent. As you can see, Gundogs vastly exceed all other dog groups, accounting for 38 per cent of all registrations, just as they did ten years ago. No other type of dog comes close in terms of popularity, and we'll be considering why that is, and how the answer might influence your choice. While Gundogs remain consistently popular, there have been some striking changes in the popularity of other groups, and we'll be looking at why that might be.

KENNEL CLUB REGISTRATION FIGURES FOR THE SEVEN DOG GROUPS		
	2015	**2006**
Gundogs	84,000	104,000
Utility	44,000	29,000
Toy	28,000	28,000
Terrier	21,000	43,000
Hound	14,000	14,000
Pastoral	14,000	21,000
Working	14,000	32,000

Gundogs

Gundogs account for over a third of all puppies registered in the UK. The group contains the world's most popular pedigree dog, the Labrador Retriever, and several other very popular breeds such as the Golden Retriever, the Springer Spaniel and the Cocker Spaniel. There are some very good reasons for the popularity of this group. Not only are its members very beautiful to look at, but they are a particularly trainable and good-tempered group of dogs. This isn't perhaps surprising when you consider that the origins of the Gundog breeds lie in their role as hunting companions working in close association with their human partners.

Origins of the Gundog

Gundogs have been bred for generations to work in close co-operation, on a one-to-one basis, with a human hunting partner. They are divided into four quite different subgroups, according to their original purpose:

- Setters and Pointers
- HPRs (Hunt-Point-Retriever)
- Spaniels
- Retrievers

The setters, HPRs and Retrievers are mostly medium to large dogs, weighing over 22.5kg (50lb) when full grown. The smaller breeds mostly belong to the Spaniel subgroup. Retrievers are single-purpose dogs bred for generations to find shot game and bring it tenderly to hand. The Spaniel's original purpose was to flush game animals from their hiding places in dense undergrowth so that they could be shot, and nowadays he is also expected to retrieve as well. The Pointers' role is to 'point out' where game birds may be hiding in wide open spaces, this allows the hunter to get within gunshot range before the bird is flushed. And finally the HPR is a Hunt-Point-Retriever who combines all the above roles into one dog. All four subgroups can make wonderful pets, but few homes can fulfil the substantial exercise needs of the beautiful Pointers and Setters.

Gundog characteristics and temperament

All Gundog breeds need a lot of exercise and some regular time spent training in order to fulfil their potential as well-behaved pets. Many Gundog breeds are very friendly, and while this is a desirable trait in a family dog, it can mean some extra time spent training your dog to be obedient around other dogs and people. Fortunately, most Gundogs are also very easy to train.

Because Gundogs have been bred to work closely with people, they tend to be very fond of human company and very keen to interact with people. This interest in co-operating with a human partner, and an ability to be trained in complex tasks, have been honed to perfection in the Retriever breeds. Together with the beauty and kind nature of the Retrievers, this has made them the most popular dogs in the world, on both sides of the Atlantic.

Several of our Gundog breeds have become deeply divided into working and non-working lines, with very little mixing of blood between the two strains. Picking which strain of dog is right for your family is an important part of the selection process, and we'll look at that more closely when we review the breeds in question. In general terms, though, if you are buying a Gundog breed as a hunting companion, it is important to buy your puppy from a breeder that specialises in working their dogs in the shooting field. Otherwise, in most cases, a show or pet-bred dog will be more suitable.

Gundog health and general care

Because Gundogs are athletic, and because many are still worked in their original roles today, Gundog breeds generally have a healthy body structure. There are a number of inherited diseases that Gundogs are susceptible to, and important health screening tests that need to be carried out on dogs that are used for breeding. We'll look at those in more detail in the Breed Reviews.

Most working-line Gundogs have fairly manageable coats, while some show lines, especially the Spaniel breeds, require more regular grooming. The HPR breeds often have short- or wire-haired coats that need minimal care.

Living with a Gundog

There are some potential disadvantages to owning a Gundog, especially a Gundog from working lines. Many Gundog breeds have strong hunting instincts and can get into bad habits chasing wildlife if not properly trained and supervised outdoors. Most are extremely bouncy when young. Many are large breeds that shed a lot of hair and enjoy getting muddy, and many have quite a doggy odour due to their oily waterproof coat. This is especially noticeable when the dog is wet. If you like an immaculate house, a Gundog is probably not your best choice. Going for a smaller breed of Gundog is not necessarily the answer for everyone, as the smaller Gundogs are Spaniels, which can be extremely lively and not particularly restful to be around. Some of these problems can be avoided by choosing a Gundog bred for the show ring or as family pets, rather than choosing a dog bred from working lines.

Gundogs have rightly earned their place as the most popular group of dogs in the world and many Gundog breeds are a great choice for active families. They are generally friendly, affectionate dogs, with little or no guarding instinct, and are capable of participating in a wide range of sports and activities.

Utility dogs

Utility dogs is the most diverse of all the groups. It contains some very well-known breeds including the iconic Bulldog, the ever popular Poodle and the beautifully marked Dalmatian. The group embraces breeds which originally served some kind of purpose, but not one that falls neatly into any of the other categories. Some of those purposes are quite obscure. The Dalmatian, for example, was originally bred to run alongside horse-drawn carriages. Many members of the Utility group have little in common with most other breeds within it, and each breed really does need to be considered on its own merits.

While registrations in several groups of dog are falling, the number of Utility group puppies increases every year. In 2006, the Utility group came fourth in the popularity stakes, well behind Gundogs, Terriers and working dogs. It accounted for just 11 per cent of all purebred puppies registered with the KC. Yet in less than a decade that number had almost doubled to 20 per cent of purebred puppies, or 44,000 puppies a year in total.

The Utility group is growing in popularity.

Utility group characteristics and temperament

Because of the disparate nature of the breeds within the group, it isn't possible to make assumptions or statements about the characteristics or needs of the breeds in this category. However, the dramatic growth in numbers of Utility group puppies being registered each year is powered by the rising popularity of just *two* breeds of dog, and they are the Bulldog and the French Bulldog.

These two breeds share a number of features in common, the most important being their physical structure. Both are short-skulled/flat-faced breeds with wonderful temperaments and great personalities and some serious health issues. The rise in popularity of the French Bulldog has been nothing short of meteoric, with registrations increasing over sevenfold in the last five years. We'll be asking why this is, and will look at how choosing such a popular breed of dog might affect you and your family in Part Two.

Toy dogs

Toy dogs are as popular as ever. The common factor running through the group is that their sole purpose has always been that of a companion. These are very small dogs, small enough to carry around in your arms or hold comfortably in your lap (hence 'lapdog'). Despite their lack of stature, many of these Toy dogs have masses of character and personality, and some breeds have very distinct characteristics, which clearly owe much to the origins of the dog.

Origins of the Toy group

Many of the Toy breeds are actually miniaturised versions of a breed from another group. So while the Yorkshire Terrier, the Italian Greyhound and the Cavalier King Charles Spaniel all belong to the Toy group, you can see from their names that their origins lie in the Terrier, Hound and Gundog groups. Some of our Toy dogs are quite ancient breeds – Pugs, for example, can be traced as far back as the sixteenth century, when individual animals were brought from China to Europe.

Toy group characteristics and temperament

Toy dogs have something of a reputation for being snappy and yappy, but this is not the full story. Many Toy dogs have very pleasant personalities. You need to look at each breed individually to make an assessment.

General health and care

Smaller dogs generally have longer lives and, while being small is not necessarily a problem when it comes to a dog's general health, there are problems with the skull, brain, eyes and teeth of some very tiny dogs. They are also frequently predisposed to knee problems and are very vulnerable to accidental injury.

Some Toy breeds have naturally manageable coats, while others have very long or profuse coats that need a great deal of grooming. If you are interested in one of the very long-coated breeds, you'll need to consider whether proper care of long fur is something you will be happy to spend your time (or money) on.

Living with a Toy dog

As discussed above, some of our Toy breeds have health problems related to structure. In addition, very small dogs are also vulnerable to injury and some Toy breeds may have uncertain temperaments, so they don't always make great pets for families with young children.

Small dogs can be big on character, and there are doubtless benefits to owning a very portable pet. Tiny dogs don't need hours of daily exercise, so you won't have to walk miles every morning even when it is pouring with rain, and many Toy dogs will adapt well to city life and to living in an apartment. Food costs and the costs of equipment such as bedding are often small, and bringing your pet Chihuahua with you when you visit friends is unlikely to make such an impact on their house party as bringing, say, a Pyrenean Mountain Dog.

Terriers

The Terriers are a group of dogs that share a common history and purpose, and as such we can look more easily at some of the characteristics and attributes of dogs that fall into this category. Terriers can be divided into two subgroups: the true Terriers, a distinctive group of mostly small, but sturdy dogs with a variety of different types of coat (smooth, wire-haired, and long); and the Bull Terriers, more muscular and more sturdily built dogs, with short, smooth coats and with distinctive blocky heads and heavier bones.

Popular Terrier breeds include the Jack Russell Terrier, recently recognised by the Kennel Club, and the Border Terrier, the UK's favourite pedigree Terrier. Terrier registrations have fallen steeply over the last few years, from over 43,000 registered births in 2006 to just over 20,000 births in 2015. A considerable proportion of this fall is accounted for by the drop in popularity of the Staffordshire Bull Terrier. We'll be looking at why this is in the Breed Review.

Origins of Terriers

The name 'Terrier' means 'of the earth', and Terriers were originally bred for various forms of vermin control, including the pursuit of their quarry underground. Many Terrier breeds are famous for their ratting skills, and others are strongly linked with the sport of foxhunting. Often each rural community would have its own breeding lines, and these were named after the location they came from. Manchester Terriers were from Manchester for example, Norfolk Terriers from Norfolk. Some Terriers have been bred with rather short legs to enable them to function more effectively below ground, but in most Terriers this has not been taken to extremes. Terriers can still be found working in the British countryside today, on farms and shoots, carrying out pest control duties just as they did a hundred years ago or more.

Bull Terriers arose when Terriers were crossed with Bulldogs – the idea being to create a dog with great courage and fighting ability to cater to the nineteenth-century enthusiasm for 'sports' such as bear- and bull-baiting. Once these sports were restricted by animal welfare laws, the focus of their owners switched to pitting dogs against one another. And although dog fighting and gambling on the outcome of a dog fight is now illegal in the UK, these activities reportedly still go on. One of our most popular Bull Terrier breeds, the Staffordshire, has had his reputation rather tarnished in the UK by an unfortunate association with illegal dog fighting and other dubious activities.

Terrier characteristics and temperament

Many of our Terrier breeds make charming pets. It is still possible to buy Terriers from working stock in rural areas and they tend to be even-tempered, likeable little dogs. Well-bred and well-socialised Bull Terriers can also make excellent pets, though The Staffordshire Bull Terrier Club notes that they are not going to be a pacifist with all other dogs. Bull Terriers have easy-care short coats, and most traditional Terrier breeds have short, manageable coats often in straight or wire varieties. Some Terrier breeds, such as the West Highland White Terrier, have a longer coat that needs a little more attention. While most Terriers are on the small side, the Airedale Terrier is a medium-to-large dog.

General health and potential problems

Terriers are mostly well-constructed little dogs that don't suffer from problems caused by structural defects. However, some of the more unusual Terriers are at risk due to their poor state of genetic health.

Some of the Working Terrier breeds can be quite vocal, and a tendency to bark may need to be discouraged from an early age in order to avoid it becoming a nuisance. If peace and quiet is your top priority, this might not be the best group for you.

Living with a Terrier

Terriers may be small, but their enthusiasm for life is huge. A Terrier can be an ideal pet for a family that doesn't have a large amount of space at home but still likes to spend plenty of active time outdoors. Short-coated Terriers don't produce the volume of hair that comes off a large dog, and are easy to keep tidy with a quick daily groom. Most Terriers will be able to accompany a family hiking or jogging, participate in active dog sports, and be on the go all day long, then curl up happily in a corner of the sofa or a small basket at the end of the day.

Hounds

Included in this group are two well-known types of Hound: Scent Hounds and Sight Hounds. Scent Hounds are mostly large, short-coated dogs with sturdy, powerful bodies, tails carried upright, long muzzles and dropped ears, often with quite long flaps. They frequently come in bold, classic Hound colours of black, white and tan, or lemon and white, with large patches of solid colour and plenty of colour on the dog's head. Many have been bred to hunt in packs and there are some Scent Hounds, such as the Basset Hound, that have been bred with shortened legs.

The Basset is a member of the Hound group of dogs.

Sight Hounds are mostly tall, slender dogs with deep narrow chests that often come in softer shades of grey, grey and white, lemon and white. They have narrow bodies and skulls, and tend to have small, semi-upright ears, with the tips folded over or back. Some Sight Hounds, like the Greyhound, are short-coated, some have coarse, wiry coats, and others, the Saluki for example, have longer silky coats.

The Hound group also includes some breeds that don't fit neatly into either of these categories. Breeds like the Dachshund and the Rhodesian Ridgeback. The Dachshund is the most popular Hound breed in the UK at the time of writing. In the USA, it is the Beagle.

Origins of the Hound

All the dogs in the Hound group were originally bred for hunting. Pack Hounds are dogs that have been bred to hunt together as a team, while remaining under the control of their human accomplices. Dogs like Beagles and Bloodhounds were bred to hunt over long distances. These are the endurance or marathon runners of the Hound group, capable of running down or wearing out their prey over a period of hours. Many Pack-Hound breeds are big dogs capable of bringing down quite large prey or holding potentially dangerous animals at bay until humans arrive to dispatch them with spears or guns.

The Sight, or 'Gaze', Hounds were bred to course their targets over shorter distances at great speed. Sight Hounds like Greyhounds and Salukis have incredibly lean and athletic bodies built for bursts of great speed. If you look at them from the front these dogs are typically very narrow, from their skull right through to their powerful hindquarters. These are the sprinters of the Hound group. There are also smaller versions of our large Sight Hounds, for example, the Italian Greyhound or the popular Whippet.

Hound characteristics and temperament

Hounds are often fairly independent dogs that are capable of remaining confident and happy without huge amounts of input from a human companion. Our Pack-Hound breeds are generally trusting and friendly towards people.

Pack Hounds can be noisy and may 'give tongue' while they are hunting – an extraordinary and spine-tingling sound outdoors in the countryside. Sight Hounds, on the other hand, are often fairly quiet, dignified dogs and somewhat introverted in nature.

General health and potential problems

The longer-legged Hounds are well-constructed dogs that can usually run, swim and climb easily and without injuring themselves. All able-bodied Hounds are active dogs and need a significant amount of daily exercise. The shorter-legged Hounds may require special care and be susceptible to back problems. Some Hounds suffer from excess skin and associated eye problems, as discussed in Chapter 4. Sight Hounds are constructed for running at speed and in general don't suffer from problems caused by poor conformation or structure.

Noise could be an issue to consider when you are thinking about the Pack-Hound breeds, and chasing can be a problem with Sight Hounds. Most Sight Hounds have powerful pursuit instincts which may be triggered by the sight of a moving object or animal. You may want to take this into account if you intend to walk your dog where there are sheep, or if your neighbours have ten cats.

Living with Hounds

Scent Hounds and Sight Hounds may belong to the same group, but they are distinctively different in many ways, and there are some Hounds that don't fall neatly into either category. You'll need to look individually at each breed that interests you, and be aware of the potential for spinal problems in the Shorter-Legged breeds.

Many Pack-Hound breeds, such as the popular Beagle, are friendly, sociable creatures that enjoy the company of other dogs and make great companions. Sight Hounds are also worth considering. Despite their size and potential for speed, these are usually gentle, placid dogs that make good-natured, quiet and unobtrusive family pets.

Pastoral dogs

The Pastoral group, known in the USA as the Herding group, contains a number of very familiar and popular breeds, as well as some quite unusual ones. Several members of this group resemble their ancestor the grey wolf in body shape, and most members are medium to large, long-legged dogs with a good length of muzzle and upright ears. The Pastoral breeds include the Border Collie, well known for its success in agility and obedience as well as being the UK's most popular working Sheepdog. And the German Shepherd Dog is a favoured service dog and the second most popular companion dog in the United States.

Origins of the Pastoral group

Pastoral dogs were originally bred for herding flocks of sheep and other livestock. Some breeds were expected to guard livestock as well as herd

The clever Border Collie belongs to the Pastoral group of dogs.

or drive it. Many breeds today still have strong herding instincts, though like Gundogs, some breeds have become divided into two strains, those bred for their original purpose and those bred specifically for the show ring. Like Gundogs, Pastoral dogs from working lines are ideally suited to work and in some cases can be more challenging for a pet owner. Choosing a dog from the right strain or line is an important part of finding the right puppy for your family.

Pastoral dog characteristics and temperament

Aside from their herding instincts, the Pastoral group contains some of our cleverest dogs. The combination of sharp intelligence together with a high degree of willingness to co-operate with a human partner has been bred into these breeds; as with Gundogs, these are characteristics required to ensure a dog can take direction at a considerable distance from his handler. Many of the Pastoral breeds are less overtly friendly than Gundogs, though, and several breeds have strong guarding instincts. Some herding breeds are also prone to chasing, and nipping at, moving objects.

General health and potential problems

With a few exceptions, the Pastoral group is a generally well-structured group of dogs. In common with many larger dogs there are inherited joint problems in some breeds, such as hip dysplasia, so it is very important to look out for the relevant health tests before purchasing a puppy. You'll find more information on this in Parts Two and Three. Having pricked ears is an advantage for many of our Pastoral dogs as upright ears enable good airflow and predisposes the dog to better ear health.

As this group can be sensitive in nature, confidence and friendliness in adult Pastoral dogs are characteristics to specifically look out for when visiting breeders.

Living with a Pastoral dog

There are many similarities between the Pastoral and Gundog groups when it comes to trainability and intelligence. They are all complex and co-operative canines. Some members of the Pastoral group can be trained to very high standards, and many Pastoral dogs seem to derive great pleasure from working as a team with a human partner. The fact that our Pastoral breeds are often less pushy, playful and outgoing in nature than their Gundog cousins can be a benefit to their owner, as it makes the dog easier to train and control in public situations where there are other dogs involved. If the idea of dog training, obedience, agility or other dog sports appeals to you, this is definitely a key group to consider.

🐾 The Working group

The purpose of the breeds within the Working group is quite varied. Consequently, the appearances and characteristics of these dogs are varied too. We have dogs as diverse as the Siberian Husky and the enduringly popular Boxer. The group also contains our large Mastiff breeds and some of our giant dogs, including the St Bernard and the Great Dane.

Origins of the Working group

Some of the dogs in the Working group, such as the Neopolitan Mastiff, were originally developed as guarding breeds, some such as the St Bernard for search-and-rescue purposes, and yet others, such as the Bernese Mountain Dog, for hauling carts and helping to herd sheep. The Greater Swiss Mountain Dog would pull carts, herd cattle and guard property too. These Working dogs are often multi-purpose breeds and many have their origins in a dog type known as the Molossers. This is a group of dogs with similar structural features that some historians believe were descended from the same ancestors. They are heavy-boned, wide-faced dogs, which include some of our giant breeds mentioned above and our powerful Mastiff breeds such as the Dogue de Bordeaux. All have relatively short muzzles and a sturdy build. The Working group also contains our ancient northern sled dogs, such as the Siberian Husky, which are altogether more athletic and wolf-like in appearance.

Working group characteristics and temperament

The variety of roles and origins of the dogs in this group makes it important to consider the temperament of each breed individually. However, many of the Molosser-type dogs in the Working group have been used for guarding purposes, and some have strong guarding instincts. Because these are mostly big dogs, with big personalities, many breeds need to be very thoroughly trained and socialised, and may benefit from an experienced handler, so they are not ideal for those short on time, or new to dogs and dog training.

Some of the sled dogs have no guarding instincts but have a reputation for being difficult to train or control off leash.

Living with a dog from the Working group

As we have seen, there is a decrease in longevity in larger breeds compared with smaller ones, and some of our very large breeds have a significantly shortened lifespan. Other health problems need to be addressed on a breed-by-breed basis. Many members of this group have well-constructed bodies from the neck down, but some have facial problems which can impair their health and lead to overheating.

This group contains a number of breeds that are popular for protection work and as guard dogs. If you are looking for a guard dog, or you are into sled racing, this is the group you'll be looking at. But for newcomers to dog ownership, this is probably not going to be your first port of call. There are some striking and beautiful dogs in this group, but it is important to understand what you are taking on before you leap into ownership. Some powerful dogs with guarding instincts are not ideally suited to life as a family pet, and most of our giant breeds have significantly short lives.

Mixed-breed dogs

Many dogs are born each year which are crossbreeds, or mixed breeds. Mixed-breeding is, of course, the 'natural' state for dogs. It is only in the last couple of hundreds of years that dogs have been segregated into separate breeds, and only in the last 100 years or so that outcrossing between breeds became taboo.

If you are considering a crossbred puppy where both parents are from the same group, then they are likely to have some of the features of that group. Many Gundog crossbreeds will have strong hunting and retrieving instincts, for example. One of the major disadvantages of buying a crossbred puppy is that you cannot be sure what he will look like, or what his abilities will be when he is grown up. Predicting the characteristics of most crosses is something of a gamble.

How do I choose?

You don't need to choose a group at this point. Indeed, you may be attracted to dogs from several different groups. But if you want a dog for a particular purpose, it may help you to focus on the group that is founded in that purpose, or to avoid a group whose members lack the attributes yours will need. If, for example, you are a keen hunter and you are looking for a hunting and shooting companion, it obviously makes sense to narrow your search down to breeds within the Gundog group. If you are looking for a dog to guard your remote homestead, then a Sight Hound won't be a good choice and a member of the Working group may suit you better. If you are looking for a family pet, then a medium-sized, friendly dog that is very interested in interacting with people is a good baseline to set. It is probably worth bearing in mind that the enduring and widespread popularity of the Gundog group is no accident, but due to the attributes they share which make them ideally suited to life in many family homes.

Remember, the descriptions and characteristics of each group do not for the most part apply to all its members. This is just a guide to help you think about the types of features you may be looking for in a dog and perhaps to help you exclude characteristics that you definitely want to avoid.

SUMMARY

- Putting a dog into groups according to its original role or purpose often tells us quite a bit about what kind of characteristics a puppy will have when he is grown up. This is important information for any puppy buyer, because, without doubt, temperament is one of the most important factors to consider when you bring a large social predator into your family. You'll find reviews of the most popular members of each of these seven groups in the next part of this book.

- In the Breed Reviews in Part Two there is information on the health, temperament, history and characteristics of each of the top 20 breeds in the UK. I also include some thoughts on their suitability as family pets, and some alternative suggestions for dogs which have problems you may want to avoid.

- Once you have found a few breeds you like the look of, you'll want to finalise your choices and get down to the serious business of finding a litter of fantastic healthy puppies, and that is what Part Three is all about. For now, it's time to investigate our most popular dogs and find out just what it is about them that makes them so irresistible!

Part Two

Breed Reviews

Introduction

White fur can be associated with hearing loss.

Each year, in the spring, the Kennel Club in the UK publishes detailed registration figures for each group of dogs and the breeds within it. In this section, I have reviewed the 20 breeds with the largest number of registered births at the time of writing, as it is likely you will be considering one or more of these for your next puppy. The information provided will also give you a clear idea of what you should know about any breed before you make a final decision on purchasing a puppy.

What is in each review?

In each review you will find an introduction to the breed and an exploration of its origins and characteristics. We'll look at the size, weight, general physical attributes and temperament of the breed. We'll examine health issues in some detail, as this is such an important factor in whether or not your dog has a long and happy life. The third section of each review covers the general grooming, exercise and other daily care needs. I'll then summarise the pros and cons of each breed and discuss its suitability as a family pet.

What kind of health data is included?

Longevity Some breeds of dog consistently live longer than others, and some consistently die younger. In the introduction to each breed I give an approximate lifespan, and you'll find the data that the lifespan figure is based on in the health

Sadly, some breeds are more susceptible to cancer than others.

section. Many books and websites claim specific lifespans for each breed, but many of these claims don't seem to be based on any kind of factual data. I have used recent health surveys and studies into canine longevity and mortality.

Cancer Many dog owners worry about cancer. It is a major disease of civilisation in both our species, especially in old age. Cancer is a leading cause of mortality in dogs, causing 27 per cent of all deaths. But there are definitely inherited tendencies to cancer – from developing cancer at a tragically young age in some breeds, while others have a much lower incidence of the disease.

Inbreeding I have also included the average coefficient of inbreeding for each breed. This figure really should be below 5 per cent (see Chapter 5) and you can check the exact coefficient of inbreeding for any litter you are interested in by using the Kennel Club Mate Select tools.

Hip scores, insurance and other health issues I also look at breed mean hip scores for some breeds, and other relevant snippets of information. And I have looked at the kind of health issues dog owners are most likely to claim for on their pet insurance when visiting a vet. The aim is to give you a general picture of the health of each breed rather than a detailed list of potential ailments.

Where does the data come from?

There are three important sources for the longevity and mortality data that is included here, together with an important source of information on brachycephalic breeds.

1. The Kennel Club Purebred Breed Health Survey 2004 (published in 2010) This was a survey of 169 of the most popular KC registered dog breeds carried out in 2004 using questionnaires sent to dog breeders. It was a joint initiative between the KC and the British Small Animal Veterinary Association and the results were published in 2010 in the Journal of Small Animal Practice. Information on over 15,000 deaths was recorded.

2. The Kennel Club Pedigree Breed Health Survey 2014 The Kennel Club carried out a repeat survey in 2014, but this time they sent questionnaires to dog owners rather than dog breeders. The results comprised a smaller number of records.

3. The longevity and mortality of owned dogs in England This third survey was published in 2013 and based on electronic patient records from veterinary practices in south-east England. Clinical data from over 100,000 dogs was analysed, including over 5,000 recorded deaths.

4. The impact of facial conformation on canine health: brachycephalic obstructive airway syndrome This study was published in Plos.one in 2015. It looks at dogs visiting the Royal Veterinary College Small Animal Hospital during the course of 2011, and compares the degree of brachycephaly (skull shortening) in each breed with the incidence of brachycephalic obstructive airway syndrome.

Full references for each survey can be found in the References and Resources chapter at the back of this book, and there are many more sources of data used in this book there too.

What is left out?

I have not listed every disease that each breed is susceptible to. There are hundreds if not thousands of inherited and/or congenital diseases found in our domestic dogs. Some are familiar to us because humans are affected too. Diseases like epilepsy and other neurological conditions, blood disorders, cancer and a range of other problems can strike dogs, and many are more common in some breeds than in others. The health information in the Breed Reviews is not an exhaustive list, simply because compiling such a list would require thousands of pages and a book far larger than this one. Instead, I have taken into consideration both the prevalence of health conditions and the effect of those conditions on the dogs' quality of life before including them here.

What you should not assume

Just because a breed is reviewed in Part Two in a positive light does not mean that all dogs belonging to that breed are destined for health and happiness.

All pedigree breeds have problems of one kind or another. It is a question of improving your odds, not of offering guarantees.

Data is helpful but should be taken in context and as an indication of potential (or lack of it) rather than a definitive answer to any concerns you may have. You can't, for example, assume that a dog with a lifespan of six years is not prone to cancer even if the cancer rate in the breed is less than 20 per cent – this is because cancer mainly affects older dogs. Nor should you assume, for example, that because a particular breed comes high in the list of long-lived dogs that your puppy will reach the same age. I have included, in some cases, the number of dogs from which data was collected, as the size of the sample is important when deciding how pertinent that information might be.

Why the emphasis on pedigree dogs?

While I do look at some popular crossbreeds at the end of the Breed Reviews, the majority of the dogs discussed here are pedigree breeds. That is partly because there is simply less information available about mixed-breed dogs, and partly because there is an infinite variety of them. It isn't possible to make generalisations or assumptions about one type of crossbreed compared with another because we don't have any evidence or data on which to base those assumptions.

SUMMARY

- As you read through the reviews, I suggest you look out for dogs that are basically structurally sound animals. Able-bodied dogs, whose conformation will not cause them distress or suffering, nor significantly shorten the expectation of a reasonable lifespan.
- The reviews are perhaps brutally honest, and in some cases you may find them disappointing, but it will save a lot of heartache in the long run if you try to avoid dogs with serious health or temperament issues.
- Keep in mind the kind of lifestyle you want to share with your dog and the reviews will help match you to the type of dog that will enjoy your needs and family situation. On top of that, I aim to reduce the chances of disaster by helping you choose breeds with a minimum of health issues and a happy, friendly temperament. Let's move on now and learn all about Britain's most popular dogs.

Breed 1

Labrador Retriever

Labrador Retrievers comprise a substantial majority of service dogs across the world including the much-loved Guide Dog For The Blind. A member of the Gundog group, Labradors are also the most popular canine hunting companion in both the UK and the USA, where they have become divided into two separate strains, those bred for work and those bred for the show ring.

Labrador registrations have fallen by around

Labradors from working lines are distinctly different from show Labs.

30 per cent in the last decade, but despite this fall the Labrador is still the most popular pet dog in the world, with over 30,000 Labrador puppies registered each year in the UK alone. This is a good-natured, well-structured, medium to large, hardy and athletic breed of dog with an easy-care short coat, and a life expectancy of 11 to 12 years.

Origins

The history of the Labrador begins in Britain. His ancestors accompanied the tough characters who crossed the world to settle in the cold wilderness of eighteenth-century Newfoundland. Then known as the St John's Dog, our Labrador's tough ancestors worked alongside fishermen in the icy waters. These dogs were then imported back to the UK, where the breed was developed into the Retriever we know and love today by two British aristocrats with a passion for shooting.

The earliest Labradors were black, with an occasional white toe or chest marks. Brown and yellow dogs were not favoured until the twentieth century was well underway, and were often culled at birth. Black dogs are still preferred in the British shooting community. The Kennel Club recognised the Labrador Retriever as a breed in 1903 and the American Kennel Club (AKC) followed later in 1917.

Breed characteristics

Bred to withstand cold weather and swim in freezing conditions, the Labrador has a thick double coat, with a warm soft underlayer and oily waterproof outer layer. The undercoat is shed and replaced regularly. The Kennel Club describes him as a strongly built and short-coupled dog (meaning the front and back legs are not too far apart), and specifies that the Labrador should stand at around 56cm (22in) at the shoulder. The adult male weighs between 29.5 and 38.5kg (65 and 85lb), depending on his breeding, and the female weighs in at some 4.5–8kg (10 to 15lb) less.

There are three recognised colours for Labrador Retrievers: yellow, black and chocolate (originally known as 'liver'), with yellow coming in a wide range of shades. Over the last 50 years, some Labradors have appeared with a gene that dilutes the three recognised colours to champagne, charcoal or silver. This dilute gene has been highly controversial, and Labradors carrying it have been rejected as not purebred by many Labrador enthusiasts.

The Labrador is one of several Gundog breeds that has become divided into two different strains with separate bloodlines. Labradors bred for work are often more sensitive than show Labs, with more powerful hunting and retrieving instincts. Bred for speed, intelligence and a co-operative nature, the field-bred Lab is often more racy and slender in appearance, and may lack the classic otter tail and chunky Labrador head. The Labrador bred for show is usually a bulkier, less agile dog and in some cases may have lightly shortened legs. The show-bred Lab may be more playful and distractible, and less intensely interested in interacting with people than his working cousins. Both strains are active and affectionate family dogs.

A key characteristic of the breed is his trusting and friendly nature. However, young Labs are powerful and bouncy dogs and can be difficult to manage alongside very small children. If you attempt to combine raising a Labrador puppy with a baby that has just started walking, you can end up spending the best part of six months picking your toddler up, drying his tears and setting him on his feet again. Many breeders won't sell Labrador puppies to families with children under five for this reason.

Most Labradors get along well with other dogs and with other family pets. However, many Labs make poor guard dogs and some rarely bark at all, so this isn't always an ideal breed for those hoping for a watchdog to chase off intruders.

Health and available screening tests

According to pet insurers Petplan, Labradors are twice as likely to need treatment for joint injuries than any other breed they insure. Major health issues in Labradors include problems such as hip and elbow dysplasia. X-rays to screen for these conditions are essential for any Labrador being used for breeding. Recent studies showed that Labradors were *less* likely to develop these joint problems (or cancer) if they were *not* neutered. Like many other breeds, Labs are also prone to progressive retinal atrophy (PRA), which causes blindness, and there is a DNA test and screening programme available for this condition.

Some of the more recent problems to appear in the breed include centronuclear myopathy (CNM), a very serious neurological condition, and exercise-induced collapse (EIC). We now have DNA tests available for these conditions, and for SD2, a form of dwarfism, and some breeders are screening their dogs for them.

Show-bred Labradors tend to have broader chests and heads.

Health statistics

The median age of death recorded for Labradors in the 2004 health survey was 12.25 years (out of 574 deaths recorded), 12.5 years in the 2013 study (418 dogs) and from the KC 2014 survey was 11 years (from 731 deaths recorded).

According to the 2004 survey, 31 per cent of Labradors die from cancer, which is slightly above average for dogs.

Average coefficient of inbreeding: 6.5 per cent. The adverse effects of inbreeding become evident when the COI of a mating exceeds 5 per cent and it is a good idea to seek out a litter with a lower COI than this.

Breed median hip score: 9. The parents of your puppy should ideally be at or below this.

Kennel Club recommended tests

The Kennel Club recommend that Labradors used for breeding are included in the following screening programmes:

- BVA/KC Hip Dysplasia Scheme
- BVA/KC/ISDS Eye Scheme
- BVA/KC Elbow Dysplasia Scheme
- DNA test – prcd-PRA.

The first two tests are obligatory for breeders who belong to the KC Assured Breeders scheme. You can also find many breeders with Labradors that have had the following:

- DNA test – CNM
- DNA test – EIC
- DNA test – SD2.

Health summary

Overall, Labrador Retrievers are soundly constructed dogs with a good chance of a healthy, happy life. There are a great many people breeding from these popular dogs but it is estimated that only around half of Labradors are currently health tested, so it is important to check health credentials for your puppy.

General care

This is a dog that needs plenty of exercise. An hour-and-a-half a day is the minimum to aim for, though your dog will be happy to walk, or work, all day long if that suits you. Exercise can be split between morning and evening, and your Labrador will cope with both cold temperatures and warm weather, provided he has plenty to drink and some shade to rest in during the hottest part of the day.

Labradors are fairly easy to train and thoroughly enjoy the process. You may need some help with walking nicely on a leash and preventing your dog from jumping up, due to his strength and friendly nature.

Mess, smell and mud are part and parcel of life with a Lab. Labradors are also a heavy-shedding breed and although their coat is easy to care for, if you want to minimise the hair being deposited on your furniture, you will need to devote some extra time to grooming the dog and vacuuming your floors. Shedding tends to be worse at certain times of the year, but many Labrador owners find there is some hair loss on a continuous daily basis. Labradors can be particularly bitey as young puppies, and boisterous and clumsy as older ones, but that phase soon passes.

Final thoughts

- The Labrador makes an outstanding family pet. These are messy, good-natured, enthusiastic dogs that love all company, both human and canine, and most will get along happily with the family cat. In addition to his superb hunting and retrieving ability, the main qualities of the Labrador are his trainable, co-operative nature, and his quick and easy intelligence. He is a robust dog who is unlikely to come to any great harm if your kids trip over him. And while he may be a poor guard dog, the other side of that coin is that he is unlikely to eat any visiting children or pets, and is a well-nigh perfect dog for an active family, where the children are all steady on their feet. This is a breed best suited to active families, where the youngest child is over five.
- Because Labradors are so popular and numerous you will have little to no trouble finding a litter. There are 13 Labrador breed clubs in the UK. The Labrador Breed Council represents them and on its website you can find links to them all. Decide which strain of Lab you want before beginning your search, as most breeders specialise in one or the other.

Breed 2

Cocker Spaniel

The field-bred Cocker has a flatter head and shorter ears.

Although small, the Cocker Spaniel is very much an outdoor dog, who loves to climb, swim, fetch a ball and get muddy. Another member of the Gundog group, working strains and show lines of Cockers are so entirely different in both temperament and appearance as to be, to all intents and purposes, two different breeds.

The Cocker Spaniel is the second most popular dog breed in the UK, and the most popular of our spaniels. Over 22,000 Cockers were registered in the UK in 2015, and registration numbers actually increased over the previous year – a reflection perhaps on the general increase in popularity of smaller dogs. This is, on the whole, a well-structured little dog with a nice temperament. The Cocker Spaniel has a lifespan of around 11 years.

Origins

Spaniels have been popular hunting companions for centuries, and were originally used simply for flushing game for falcons or into nets. Once guns arrived on the scene, flushing Spaniels were used to produce game for the gun. Cocker Spaniels and Springer Spaniels were once simply divided by weight – the name 'Cocker' refers to the woodcock, one of the edible gamebirds which the working Cocker is expected to flush for the gun – but over the intervening years they have become two distinctive breeds with individual personalities – Cockers were recognised as a separate breed from Springers and Field Spaniels in 1873.

Over the last 50 years, the Cocker has become divided into two types, show and field, each with its own distinct bloodlines and, unlike Retriever breeds, the two strains are almost never mixed.

Breed characteristics

The Kennel Club describes the Cocker Spaniel as a 'merry' little dog. Both show and working Cockers are happy, friendly, affectionate little dogs, but that's about where the similarities end. The show Cocker's coat can be profuse and may need a lot of grooming. His ears are long and low-set, his head domed and his expression solemn. He is as tall as he is long, weighs in at 12.5–14.5kg (28–32lb) and stands 38–40.5cm (15–16in) tall.

Working-strain Cockers tend to be a little smaller and commonly weigh around 10–12.5kg (22–28lb). The working Cocker has a flatter head; much shorter, higher-set ears than his show-bred cousin; and tight button eyes with no trace of solemnity. He has a shorter, easier-to-manage coat, which may be quite curly in places, and has a tendency to be a little longer in the body than he is tall.

Cocker Spaniels come in the most bewildering array of colours. From jet black or brown, through rich red, to orange and palest lemon. There are also varieties with patches of these colours on a white background, or speckled roan versions – pretty much a colour to suit everyone. This is a shedding breed and will involve you in a certain amount of vacuuming!

It is important to be aware of the difference in temperament between the two strains of Cocker. The working Cocker is a veritable powerhouse of energy. This is a dog that can hunt all day and yet be small enough to cuddle up on your lap in the evening. He can jump many times his own height, swim considerable distances and do either of these things while carrying a large bird or rabbit in his mouth. He is a very determined character that is resistant to discomfort and desperate to hunt. Although the Cocker's primary function is to find and flush game, the modern working Cocker is also a superb retriever, working to whistle and hand signals where necessary.

The show Cocker is a more relaxed and easy-going character. He is happy to fetch a ball but doesn't think the world will end if he can't find it. He is content to trot along sniffing where a rabbit has been but doesn't feel the need to do so at breakneck speed. His pace of life is gentler, and your walks together should be relaxing rather than frantic.

Health and available screening tests

Cocker Spaniels suffer from a number of health conditions, including hip dysplasia and progressive retinal atrophy (PRA). They also suffer from an inherited form of glaucoma, and from familial nephropathy (FN), a progressive kidney disease. More recently, an unpleasant condition called acral mutilation syndrome (AMS) has been shown to affect Cockers. Affected dogs have altered sensation in their extremities and may mutilate themselves – a DNA test is now available for this disease. According to Petplan, Cockers are twice as likely to need treatment for eye conditions as any other breed. Long droopy ears are always prone to problems and the most common health problem Cockers are treated for is inflammation of the outer ear.

There are a number of screening programmes available for Cocker breeders. The Working Spaniel community are still some way behind in this respect, and at the time of writing it is easier to find a fully health-tested, show-bred Cocker than one from working lines.

Show-bred Cocker Spaniels have very long ears and a solemn expression.

Health statistics

Both the 2004 and the 2014 pedigree health surveys agree on a lifespan of 11 years for this little dog. The death rate from cancer is at 29 per cent, only slightly above average for a dog.

Average coefficient of inbreeding: 9.6 per cent. Many working Cocker pairings have a higher COI than this. You can use the online working Cocker database to help you find a better mating. The adverse effects of inbreeding become evident when the COI of a mating exceeds 5 per cent and it is a good idea to seek out a litter with a lower COI than this.

Breed median hip score for Cocker Spaniels: 10. The parents of your puppy should ideally be at or below this.

Kennel Club recommended health tests

- BVA/KC/ISDS Eye Scheme
- DNA test – prcd-PRA
- DNA test – FN
- BVA/KC Hip Dysplasia Scheme
- BVA/KC/ISDS Gonioscopy.

The first three are obligatory for Kennel Club Assured Breeders with HD and Gonioscopy being recommended. They recommend you also consider:

- DNA test – AMS.

Health summary

This is a basically healthy breed with tests available for the inherited conditions that are currently a cause for concern. It will be harder to find a fully health-screened Cocker Spaniel if you are looking for a dog from working lines.

General care

Cockers need a minimum of an hour or so of exercise each day. Working-strain Cockers will benefit from more than this, and need to be supervised and engaged with outdoors. Retrieving games and swimming are great exercise options for this breed. These are intelligent dogs that get bored easily and all will benefit enormously from daily training sessions.

Ear infections are always a problem in floppy-eared dogs, and ear care is important in long-eared Spaniels. Working Cockers have shorter and more mobile ears but are still prone to infection and general grubbiness, so regular ear inspections need to be a part of your grooming regime.

The longer fur around a Spaniel's rear end, ears and in his armpits is prone to matting if not combed thoroughly from time to time. This is not a breed where you can get away with a weekly brushing, you need to groom regularly, ideally on a daily basis, especially with a show-bred dog.

Final thoughts

- If you are interested in a Cocker Spaniel as a pet, your first step should be to determine what strain of Cocker you would like. Fifty years ago, working strains of the Cocker Spaniel were on the brink of extinction. In recent years, the working Cocker has made a huge comeback, and increasingly is found in our homes as pets and companions, but working Cockers are not ideally suited to every family. Be aware that if exercised outdoors *without much input from the owner*, in areas where wild animals are abundant, working Cockers can be difficult to control.

- Most Cockers are kind and gentle with children, big enough to cope with little ones and small enough not to knock them flying. The quick and agile working Cocker is a great choice for those who are interested in Gundog work or in agility; he also excels at tracking and competitive obedience. For those looking purely for a family pet, the show Cocker with his calmer temperament is often a better choice, and less likely to give his owner heart failure by relentlessly pursuing the local wildlife from one end of the county to the other.

- All Cockers love to be outdoors whatever the weather and make great hiking or jogging companions. There are over 20 Cocker Spaniel clubs in the UK; some cover both working and show strains, a few are specifically for the working dog. They are all listed on the Kennel Club website.

Breed 3

French Bulldog

A member of the Utility group of dogs, the French Bulldog is a small, compact Bulldog with plenty of character, a broad chest and distinctive large, upright ears. He is also a dog that is currently taking the world by storm. In 2006 there were just over 500 French Bulldog births registered in the UK. In 2015 the number was over 14,000. Births had increased by over 50 per cent from the previous year. Right now, the French Bulldog looks unstoppable!

This dog belongs to the brachycephalic (flat-faced) category we talked about in Chapter 4, which means he has some serious health issues to contend with. His life expectancy is around nine years.

The French Bulldog is experiencing a meteoric rise in popularity.

Origins

The French Bulldog is actually English in origin. In 1835 bull and bear baiting was outlawed in England, and the role of Bull breeds shifted, with smaller Bulldogs becoming popular as pets. The French Bulldog is descended from a strain of small Bulldog that was said to have been popular with lacemakers in the Nottingham area. When these lacemakers emigrated to France in search of work, they took their little dogs with them. Some of those early dogs had the tipped-over 'rose' ears we see in the Bulldog; others had erect ears. Over time, upright ears became more popular and enthusiasts who established the breed in the USA made the French Bulldog's distinctive bat ears part of the breed standard. Breed numbers declined during the Depression of the 1930s and did not significantly recover until the 1980s. Thirty years later, the French Bulldog began to accelerate in popularity and is now probably the fastest-growing breed in the world.

The French Bulldog today looks a little different from his forebears. Over the years, the French Bulldog breeders have selected for shorter muzzles and an increasingly flat face.

Breed characteristics

The Kennel Club breed standard describes a solid, small dog with bat ears and a short tail. The KC standard requires that the eyes should be moderated in size and not prominent, but like all brachycephalic dogs, bulging eyes are not uncommon in the breed. Male French Bulldogs generally weight up to 12.5kg (28lb), with female dogs weighing in at around 2kg (4lb) lighter. Most Frenchies are around 30cm (12in) in height. The coat is short and smooth, and only three colours are permitted in the show ring – brindle, fawn and pied (which includes white). Other colours, though popular with some members of the public, are considered highly undesirable by show breeders.

The Kennel Club states early on in the breed standard that signs of respiratory distress are undesirable. This reference to breathing is an unusual inclusion in a breed standard, and a reflection of the problems that exist within the breed. The breed standard also asks for a well-defined muzzle, and here is where the problems start. Photos of French Bulldogs from the early 1900s show that they had open nostrils and a short muzzle. But many Frenchies today have little or no muzzle to speak of. This is a change that has crept into the breed over the last few decades and is a matter for increasing concern among veterinary professionals.

This is a deeply affectionate and very charming companion breed. Owners describe them as quiet, attentive and playful. The French Bulldog is not yappy, and though some Frenchies aren't especially fond of other dogs, they are generally very friendly towards people. The delightful character of the French Bulldog goes some way to explaining the enormous increase in interest in these little dogs. Sadly, all is not well in the health department.

Health and available screening tests

The French Bulldog is a brachycephalic (short-faced) breed with chondrodystrophy (a form of dwarfism). We discussed the problems caused by brachycephaly and chondrodystrophy in Chapter 4 – most importantly, brachycephaly causes a host of serious health problems, including brachycephalic obstructive airway syndrome (BOAS), which interferes with breathing, causing great distress to the dog, and which can be fatal. A study published in 2015 showed that BOAS increases proportionately to decreasing skull length. It also showed that the French Bulldog was at second-highest risk of any breed (after the Pug). Gagging, regurgitation, vomiting and a range of eye problems are also associated with brachycephaly. Clinical signs can be severe by 12 months of age. Like all brachycephalic dogs, French Bulldogs are prone to dental problems due to over-crowded teeth in their shortened jaws.

The French Bulldog is also susceptible to intervertebral disk disease (IVDD) as a result of its dwarfism, and to hereditary cataracts (HC). According to a recent VetCompass study, the Frenchie is one of the three breeds most likely to suffer from patellar luxation (kneecaps popping out of joint), especially if individuals are particularly small, female or neutered.

This is a breed with large shoulders, broad heads and narrow hips, and birthing difficulties are common.

Health statistics

The 2004 health survey, which looked at over 70 deaths, recorded a median age of just nine years. For a relatively small dog this is poor – many small breeds live far longer. The commonest cause of death recorded in the 2014 health survey was heart failure followed by cancer, which has an above average risk in this breed too, with an incidence of 38 per cent.

Average coefficient of inbreeding: 3.5 per cent. The adverse effects of inbreeding become evident when the COI of a mating exceeds 5 per cent and it is a good idea to seek out a litter with a lower COI than this.

Kennel Club recommended tests

The Kennel Club recommend the following health tests for French Bulldogs:

- BVA/KC/ISDS Eye Scheme
- DNA test – HC-HSF4
- Participation in the French Bulldog Health Scheme.

Health summary

All French Bulldogs have brachycephaly, and if you decide to own a Frenchie you and your dog will have to live with the side effects of this condition, including your dog's inability to cool himself. If your heart is set on a French Bulldog, then you should consider seeking lines with as much visible muzzle as possible. It may also help if you find a breeder who participates in the French Bulldog Health Scheme, which offers a series of graded certificates of health, including respiratory tests and assessments by a qualified veterinary surgeon. Sadly, the only way to avoid the problems that beset this breed entirely is to choose a different breed of dog. French Bulldogs can be difficult or expensive to insure due to their medical problems – I approached five insurance companies and two refused to quote for this breed.

General care

The French Bulldog has an easy-care coat and needs minimal brushing, but he does need a lot of skincare because the folds on his face and the area around his tail are prone to infection. You will need to clean the skinfolds on your Frenchie's face carefully every day or they will become smelly and sore. If he has a screw tail, the same applies to his bottom, which he may need help in keeping clean. You'll also need to clean your French Bulldog's teeth daily, as overcrowded teeth are very vulnerable to infection and decay.

Like all dogs, your French Bulldog will need regular exercise, but there are some important safety considerations when exercising a Frenchie. One is safety around water. It is very important to recognise that many French Bulldogs cannot swim, and can drown in shallow water. Another consideration is safety when excited or whenever respiration rate increases. Increased respiration puts pressure on an already struggling airway system. Many Frenchies find it hard to oxygenate themselves effectively during prolonged exercise, and some will need to be restricted to short walks. In addition, brachycephalic dogs cannot cool themselves effectively and easily overheat in warm weather. It is very important to read up on BOAS before you purchase a brachycephalic puppy. Symptoms are often missed, and early diagnosis is vital if surgery is to be effective.

Final thoughts

- This is not a dog for anyone who likes to go running or on long walks and wants a dog to go with them. Many Frenchies are unable to exercise vigorously for long. You must be able to keep a Frenchie cool in warm weather and to recognise symptoms of respiratory distress.
- It isn't difficult to find a French Bulldog puppy, though the prices charged are often double what you would pay for a puppy of another breed and this is partly because of demand, but also partly because most Frenchies need a caesarean section to deliver their puppies safely.
- Despite their undoubted charm and immense appeal, this is a breed with special needs. While some French Bulldogs remain in reasonable health, there are undoubtedly others that suffer greatly due to the facial structure that breeders have provided for them. With such poor health prospects, I am unable to recommend the French Bulldog as a suitable companion dog. Some alternative small breeds in better health are the Border Terrier, the Miniature Schnauzer and the Miniature Poodle. If a short coat or a Bull breed is the main appeal, you might like to consider a Staffordshire Bull Terrier, a slightly larger but healthier breed.

Breed 4

English Springer Spaniel

The Springer is a lively dog.

A member of our Gundog group of dogs, the English Springer Spaniel is one of the most popular and competent shooting companions available in the UK today. A very attractive Spaniel, with his black-and-white or liver-and-white patched coat, the Springer is also currently the fourth most popular pet dog in the UK. This is a divided breed, with separate working and show bloodlines that are a little different in appearance and very different in personality.

Only five breeds of dog in the UK produce over 10,000 puppies a year, and the Springer is one of them. But Springer numbers have been declining steadily over the last ten years, down from over 15,000 in 2006. This is probably partly a reflection of the trend towards smaller dogs, and partly a reflection of the general decrease in dog registrations.

The Springer is an active, well-constructed and generally healthy breed. Not only is the Springer a popular pet, but due to his splendid sense of smell, intelligence and trainability, he is also much in demand as a service dog. He has a lifespan of 11 to 12 years.

Origins

A British breed, the English Springer Spaniel traces his origins back to the flushing Spaniels we see in eighteenth-century paintings. Spaniels were at one time divided into land and water Spaniels, with the Springer or Springing Spaniel belonging to the former group. Originally known as the Norfolk Spaniel, the breed was officially recognised by the Kennel Club in 1902. Flushing Spaniels have been used as working Gundogs in Britain since the earliest days of shooting.

Not that long ago, the Springer and the Cocker were essentially one breed and were allocated to one group or the other by their weight. Over recent dog generations, the two have become distinctly separate breeds with their own personalities and hunting styles. More recently, the English Springer Spaniel has become completely divided into two separate strains, work and show. The temperament of these two strains of Springer differs widely, and the show strain of Springer is often better suited to the average pet owner than his working-bred relatives.

Breed characteristics

The Kennel Club describes the Springer as the longest-legged and raciest of the British land Spaniels. This is a fairly deep-chested, broad-skulled dog reaching 51cm (20in) at the shoulder. The show Springer has a large domed head and low-set, very long ears. This gives him a rather solemn expression. The working-strain dog has shorter, more mobile ears and a flatter head. There is considerable variation in size. Show dogs can be quite large and solidly built, with the working strains often much smaller and far more agile dogs. The adult show Springer can weigh as much as 22.5kg (50lb) with his working cousins 4.5–7kg (10–15lb) lighter; females a little less for both.

Traditionally, the English Springer comes in just two colours – liver and white or black and white. The show variety also permits tan markings on either of the above, but doesn't allow roan versions, and the patches need to be of solid colour. Working strains often come with plenty of speckles, and some are almost roan in appearance. Both types have a weather-resistant and moderately feathered coat that sheds.

The Springer has an amazing sense of smell and loves nothing better than to follow a scent trail. The Kennel Club describes 'A friendly, happy dog . . . with an alert, kind expression', and Springers are indeed generally friendly dogs, but not in such a pushy way as Labradors and some Cockers can be. They are happy to receive a pat from a stranger, but probably won't try to climb in his lap. Working-strain Springers have more natural hunting drive and may be quick to learn, but can be more challenging to control. There are some temperament issues in some working lines of English Springer, with obsessive behaviour such as light chasing occasionally cropping up. In homes where supervision and training are not provided, working-bred Springers can become hyperactive in the house and bolting (running away) outdoors can be a serious issue.

On the whole, the breed is a friendly, happy, even-tempered one that fits in well with family life. Laid-back individuals from working lines can be found, but on the whole, the show-bred Springer is a more tranquil character.

Show Springer Spaniels tend to be a little calmer than their working cousins.

Health and available screening tests

English Springer Spaniels suffer from joint problems, including hip and elbow dysplasia. According to Petplan, joint problems are the second most common problem that they see in this Spaniel breed. They are also susceptible to progressive retinal atrophy, glaucoma, and to fucosidosis (Fuco) and phosphofructokinase disease (PFK). Fucosidosis is a severe, progressive and fatal neurological disease, while PFK causes exercise intolerance and a range of clinical symptoms such as anaemia and jaundice. DNA tests have now been developed for these conditions. You may find it more difficult to find a fully health-tested Springer from working lines, as to date the show community have made much more effort to implement these tests.

Health summary

The 2004 health survey records the median age at death for a Springer Spaniel as 12 years. The KC 2014 survey puts this at 11 years. The 2004 survey records that 26.7 per cent of English Springers die from cancer – about average for a dog.

Average coefficient of inbreeding: 9.7 per cent. The adverse effects of inbreeding become evident when the COI of a mating exceeds 5 per cent and it is a good idea to seek out a litter with a lower COI than this.

Breed median hip score: ten. The parents of your puppy should ideally be at or below this.

Kennel Club recommended tests

- BVA/KC/ISDS Eye Scheme
- DNA test – PRA (cord1)
- BVA/KC/ISDS Gonioscopy
- DNA test – Fuco
- BVA/KC Hip Dysplasia Scheme
- DNA test – PFK.

The first four tests are compulsory for Kennel Club Assured Breeders and the last two are highly recommended.

Health summary

This is a basically healthy breed with tests available for the inherited conditions that are currently a cause for concern. It will be harder to find a fully health-screened Springer Spaniel if you are looking for a dog from working lines.

General care

The English Springer Spaniel is a clever, active dog, who will look for entertainment elsewhere if you don't provide it. This is especially true of working-strain dogs, but all Springers need plenty of exercise and mental stimulation. A mixture of long walks and retrieving games is ideal for a show Springer. A working-line dog will need more supervision and training, ideally Gundog-style training, in order to keep him fit, happy and under your control.

Although they don't have an excessively heavy coat, Springers need daily grooming, with particular attention paid to ear flap, 'trousers' and chest hair. If you don't do this, you'll end up with a matted dog. Attention to ears beneath the flaps is also important. Like many Gundog breeds the Springer has a distinctive doggy odour, especially when wet.

Final thoughts

- The Springer Spaniel is a robust, medium-sized dog that will be able to participate in pretty much any activity his family can dream up. Most Springers are affectionate without being clingy, easy to train, active dogs that won't eat you out of house and home, and are good with children. This is a dog who will fetch a ball or a Frisbee from dawn till dusk, bark at intruders but not bite them, and live a long and healthy life. Unless you specifically want a working Gundog or a Springer that will compete in agility, many people will be happier with the more relaxed and less-driven temperament of the show Springer as a family pet.

- If you don't mind a little time daily spent grooming and training, and a good long walk each day, this could be the dog for you. The main problem that people experience with Springers is control issues out-doors, and these problems tend to be largely confined to the working Springer.

- There are plenty of Springer litters available during the summer months, so you shouldn't have too much trouble finding a puppy. You can find Springer breeders through your local club – there are ten breed clubs listed on the Kennel Club website. If you want a working dog, you need to contact the Kennel Club's Field Trial secretary.

Breed 5

Pug

Pugs have grown hugely in popularity in recent years.

nstantly recognisable, with his characterful, almost human features, the Pug is the most popular member the Toy group. A chunky little dog with a curled tail, he has a long history and has often been associated with royalty. Over 10,000 Pug puppies are born each year, and at the current rate of growth the Pug is likely to overtake the Springer Spaniel and become our fourth most popular dog breed. The Pug suffers from a range of health disorders associated with his structure and he is not a particularly long-lived dog for his size, with an average lifespan of 11 years.

Origins

Bred purely as a companion, the Pug is a particularly ancient breed. We don't know for sure, but it seems likely that the Pug is oriental in origin, then made its way to Europe, where the breed was adopted by several royal families. Anecdotes about Pugs go back hundreds of years. William, Prince of Orange is said to have been warned of approaching Spaniards by his Pug in 1572, and the French Empress Josephine is said to have owned a Pug called Fortune, who reportedly bit Napoleon Bonaparte on their wedding night. In the 1860s, British soldiers brought a number of Pugs back to England from China and in 1866 the first black Pug was seen in England.

The Pug has always been a short-nosed dog, but in recent years the breed has become increasingly flat-faced. If we look at the famous self-portrait by William Hogarth (1745), which includes his Pug, Trump, it is clear that the dog in the painting has a distinct, though short, muzzle. This is not the case for many Pugs today.

Breed characteristics

The Kennel Club describes the Pug as 'decidedly square and cobby'. His large eyes are set into a wrinkled, flattened face that gives him the almost human look that people find so attractive and amusing. At just 25.5–30cm (10–12in) tall, this is a small dog but no lightweight for his size: he weighs 6.5–8kg (14–18lb) and is solidly built. Most Pugs are fawn in colour, with a black or dark mask and ears. Some Pugs have a 'trace' or line of dark fur running the length of their back. Other permitted colours are black, silver and apricot. Apart from black, sometimes it is difficult to tell what colour a puppy is going to be at birth as the colour differences are subtle and a puppy's fur may darken or lighten as it gets older. Some black Pugs (not all) have a single coat and shed less than their fawn cousins.

Many people think that Pugs naturally make a snorting noise when they are breathing, or have heard that Pugs snore loudly. These are actually symptoms of the respiratory problems that are common in the breed and should never be ignored. This is a friendly, even-tempered breed, not yappy or aggressive. Sometimes described as low-energy or even lazy, this is more a reflection of the Pug's poor ability to oxygenate himself rather than any lack of enthusiasm on his part.

🐾 Health and available screening tests

The Pug has serious health issues related to his structure. The very flat face makes it difficult for a Pug to breathe easily or to cool himself. This is the breed with the least muzzle, and not unsurprisingly the breed most likely to suffer from brachycephalic obstructive airway syndrome (BOAS) and its associated breathing problems. A study in 2015 found that 88 per cent of Pugs suffered from BOAS. In a follow-up study, a shocking 91 per cent of Pugs were diagnosed with the disorder. Breathing problems are the third most common reason for Pugs to need veterinary treatment (Petplan). You can find out more about brachycephaly and its complications in Chapter 4, but common symptoms of respiratory distress in Pugs are noisy breathing, fainting, trying to sleep sitting up, neck stretching, and low energy or reluctance to exercise. Gagging, regurgitation, vomiting, skinfold infections and a range of eye problems are also associated with the breed. According to Petplan, Pugs are more likely to need treatment for eye problems than for any other reasons, and the commonest health condition recorded in the 2014 health survey was corneal ulcers, a painful condition caused by the Pug's brachycephalic skull, which makes the eyes protrude.

In common with other curly-tailed dogs, Pugs can also suffer from hemivertebrae (see Chapter 4), which can cause painful back problems, a form of encephalitis (PDE), and like many Toy dogs, they suffer from patellar luxation (kneecaps popping out of joint). There are schemes available to screen for these conditions.

Health statistics

The median age of death for Pugs recorded in the 2004 health survey (out of 163 deaths in total) was 11 years.

Average coefficient of inbreeding: 5.7 per cent. The adverse effects of inbreeding become evident when the COI of a mating exceeds 5 per cent and it is a good idea to seek out a litter with a lower COI than this.

The Pug is a category 3 breed on the Kennel Club's Breed Watch scheme. This is a scheme to help judges be alert to signs that a dog is suffering, or has suffered in the past, from conditions related to his body structure or conformation.

Points of special concern for Pugs include:

- **Difficulty breathing**
- **Excessive nasal folds**
- **Excessively prominent eyes**

- Hair loss or scarring from dermatitis
- Incomplete blink
- Pinched nostrils
- Significantly overweight
- Signs of dermatitis in skinfolds
- Sore eyes due to damage or poor eyelid conformation
- Unsound movement.

Kennel Club recommended tests

The Kennel Club recommends that Pug breeders participate in the following scheme:

- Breed Council – hemivertebrae checking
- Additional tests commonly in use by breeders in the UK
- Patellar luxation
- DNA test – PDE.

Health summary

All Pugs have brachycephaly, and if you decide to own a Pug you and your dog will have to live with the side effects of this condition, including your dog's inability to cool himself. If your heart is set on a Pug, then you should consider seeking lines with as much visible muzzle as possible. Overall, this is a troubled breed with a significant chance of distressing health problems. Puppy buyers need to acquaint themselves with the problems associated with brachycephaly before making a commitment to a dog of this breed.

General care

Brachycephaly is a disability and brachycephalic dogs need extra care when exercising, especially outdoors. Like most brachycephalic dogs, many Pugs cannot swim or can only swim for short periods of time and with difficulty, so you must never leave your Pug unsupervised near water. Pugs also have great difficulty cooling themselves and should never be exercised in warm weather or left outside without access to a cool place to lie. This is not a breed for joggers or marathon runners, and heatstroke or respiratory distress can come on rapidly if your Pug is allowed to get out of breath in warm conditions. His coat requires only minimal grooming, but like all dogs with skinfolds, the Pug's must be kept clean and dried off after bathing. He may also need some help in keeping his bottom clean. You'll also need to clean your Pug's teeth daily, as overcrowded teeth are very vulnerable to infection and decay.

These are clever little dogs who enjoy training, spending time with people and being active. But if you intend to own a Pug you must pay attention to the temperature and know how to spot symptoms of respiratory distress.

Final thoughts

- This is a wonderfully characterful and affectionate little dog that really deserves a better deal than the one he currently has health-wise. The plight of the Pug is recognised by the Kennel Club through their inclusion of the breed in category 3 of their Breed Watch scheme, but sadly no minimum muzzle length is required or recommended by the Kennel Club at the present time. For those who want a small dog, healthier alternatives to the Pug are the Toy Poodle and the Border Terrier. But if your heart is set on a Pug puppy, try to find a breeder with Pugs whose noses project beyond that nose roll that sits above the nostrils. Even a small amount of muzzle will help your dog to breathe and cool himself more effectively.
- It isn't possible for me to recommend the Pug as a pet dog at this time. I very much hope changes will be made to the breed standard in the future, but at the moment this is a little dog with big problems.

Breed 6

German Shepherd Dog

The German Shepherd Dog (GSD) is a member of the Pastoral group of dogs. Well known for his role as a military service dog, the beautiful GSD was a hero breed in my childhood, when virtually all working police dogs were German Shepherds. Like so many breeds, the German Shepherd Dog has seen a big decline in numbers in the last few years, dropping from over 12,000 puppies registered in 2006 to under 8,000 in 2015. Again, there are probably several factors involved, including the public concerns about exaggerations and health, which we'll look at below, and the growing trend towards smaller, flatter-faced dogs. This is a breed with a lifespan of ten to 11 years.

German Shepherd Dogs can make excellent companions and are easily trained.

The German Shepherd dog is a highly intelligent dog with some guarding instincts.

🐾 Origins

The German Shepherd Dog was created by a group of enthusiasts led by a man called Max von Stephanitz in Germany in the 1890s. Von Stephanitz, a career soldier with extensive veterinary knowledge, wanted to try to create the ultimate all-purpose herding dog. Founding the German Shepherd Dog Club, according to the Nova Scotia GSD Club his motto was 'utility and intelligence'. He also developed a series of tests to help ensure the breed retained its working abilities, and actively encouraged the use of his new breed as a service dog. In the UK,

54 German Shepherd Dogs were recognised by the Kennel Club in 1919 and this figure swelled to 8,000 by 1926. Recognised by the American Kennel Club in 1908, the German Shepherd is now the second most popular breed in the USA.

During the early part of the twentieth century, the main role of the breed shifted from herding and guarding livestock to service and protection work. The First World War saw the GSD established as a valuable service dog to the armed forces, with over 48,000 German Shepherds serving in the German army. By the 1960s the German Shepherd Dog had already forged a place as the most sought after police and military service dog in the world.

Breed characteristics

The German Shepherd Dog is a prick-eared, wolf-shaped dog with a powerful body, thick coat and long, tapered muzzle. He is slightly longer in the body than he is tall, and stands at about 63.5cm (25in) high – 58.5cm (23in) for females. The Kennel Club breed standard describes a versatile working dog, and states that he should be balanced and free from exaggeration. It describes a topline that 'runs without any visible break from the set on of the neck, over the well-defined withers, falling away slightly in a straight line to the gently sloping croup.' This particular point is the subject of much debate, as we'll see below. An adult male GSD can be expected to weight 29.5–41kg (65–90lb), with females coming in 4.5–7kg (10–15lb) lighter. This is a shedding breed and the German Shepherd's thick double coat comes in the familiar gold or tan with a dark saddle, but can also be found in solid black and black with lighter markings. Solid white or liver is considered highly undesirable by the Kennel Club. There is also the long-haired version in the same colours.

Like some of our Gundog breeds, the German Shepherd Dog has become split into two different types, and if you want a GSD you need to decide which type is right for you. We looked at the structural problems that can be found in German Shepherds in both Europe and America in Chapter 4, so you will be aware that there is a concern that many GSD show breeders are not interpreting the breed standard, with regard to topline, in the way intended by the Kennel Club. For this reason, the German Shepherd Dog has been placed in category 3 in the Kennel Club's Breed Watch scheme. The problem is that rear-leg angulation has been taken too far in some GSD lines, causing weakness and instability in the hindquarters of the affected dogs. However, there *are* well-constructed GSDs out there, being bred by enthusiasts for a healthier dog and by some of those competing in sports such as working trials and agility. Your best way to find those dogs is to search for breeders who produce more level-backed dogs that compete in athletic events, and to avoid show-line dogs until the situation improves, which hopefully it will do in the future.

The German Shepherd Dog is a naturally protective breed and develops a deep bond with his trainer. He should be loyal, brave and confident. Like many Pastoral breeds, German Shepherds are not expected to be especially playful or friendly towards total strangers, nor should they be overly shy or show any trace of nerves. If trained correctly, many GSDs have the potential temperament to make a formidable guard dog – those who intend to harness this potential need to be knowledgeable, skilful and in full control of the dog at all times. Like all guarding breeds, German Shepherd Dogs need extensive socialisation and training to ensure that they are safe and well-mannered domestic companions.

Health and available screening tests

German Shepherd Dogs suffer from hip dysplasia, elbow dysplasia, eye diseases and a neurological condition – degenerative myelopathy (DM), which affects the spine of older dogs. Less well known, but also found in the breed, is an inherited form of pituitary dwarfism (PD), which produces a small dog with normal proportions; a faulty gene that can cause adverse reactions to common drugs (MDR1); and a condition called mucopolysaccharidosis (MPS) that causes skeletal problems at an early age. There are tests available for these conditions. Haemophilia is also a problem in the breed, but it can usually be treated and there is a testing scheme available. According to Petplan, German Shepherds are particularly at risk from haemangiosarcoma, a rapidly growing cancer of the blood vessels.

At the time of writing, the GSD is listed as a category 3 dog on the Kennel Club's Breed Watch scheme. Here are the problems the Kennel Club are concerned about:

- **Cow hocks**
- **Excessive turn of stifle**
- **Nervous temperament**
- **Sickle hock**
- **Weak hindquarters.**

Health statistics

According to the 2004 health survey, less than 2 per cent of the 1,400 questionnaires sent to the British Association for German Shepherd Dogs during the collection of data were returned, and they were therefore sadly excluded from the results. However, the 2013 study records a median age at death of 11 years for the breed, with the 2014 health survey recording a median age at death of ten years.

Average coefficient of inbreeding: 3.2 per cent. The adverse effects of inbreeding become evident when the COI of a mating exceeds 5 per cent and it is a good idea to seek out a litter with a lower COI than this.

Kennel Club recommended tests

- **BVA/KC Hip Dysplasia Scheme**
- **BVA/KC Elbow Dysplasia Scheme**
- **BVA/KC/ISDS Eye Scheme**
- **Breed Club – Haemophilia testing for males.**

Only the first of these is obligatory for KC Assured Breeders. Other tests available for consideration include:

- **DNA test – DM**
- **DNA test – PD**
- **DNA test – MDR1**
- **DNA test – MPS**

Health summary

This is a potentially fairly healthy breed but there are structural problems in some show lines.

General care

This is a dog bred for outdoor work and physically demanding exercise. He is also immensely intelligent and easily bored. Most days he will need the best part of a couple of hours' exercise, and once adult will thoroughly enjoy long hikes. Some of his exercise needs can be accommodated in training exercises such as ball games, retrieves and tug games, but this is not a dog for someone who doesn't like walking. With any powerful dog, especially one that has guarding instincts, regular daily training sessions will build the bond you need between you and help you set out behaviour guidelines and keep your dog under control, and the GSD is no different.

This is a shedding breed, with a thick, medium-length coat. It doesn't tangle easily or need a massive amount of grooming. However, when your GSD is shedding, grooming will help cut down on the hair floating around your home and so it is important that he is happy to be thoroughly brushed. A quick daily brush as a puppy should help get him used to being groomed, and twice weekly as an adult will keep his coat tidy. Long-haired GSDs need a regular daily brushing.

Final thoughts

- According to the German Shepherd Dog Rescue, nervous aggression is becoming more common in the breed, and as with any large powerful breed of dog, especially one with a guarding instinct, temperament is paramount. The careful choice of puppy needs to include close scrutiny of the parents, who should be calm, unafraid of visitors and happy to meet you and make friends.
- A powerful herding dog with a strong guarding instinct, the breed is one of the most popular family pets in the world. While some breeders of GSDs are giving the Kennel Club and the wider public such cause for concern, there are also German Shepherd enthusiasts who are breeding for a straight or level topline and who are also health testing their dogs. This means it is possible to buy a well-constructed GSD in the UK if you are prepared to do some research and pick your breeder carefully.
- If you find the right lines, this is an excellent all-round family dog who will love being trained for obedience or to help you explore the world of working trials or agility. He will act as a watchdog and be happy to go jogging or hiking with you, and will give you ten years or more of loyal friendship.
- If you love the look of the breed and are struggling to find level-backed lines, an alternative breed to consider is the Belgian Malinois, which is also increasingly popular as a service dog. The population is small, but the breed is well constructed, has a lower-than-average rate of cancer and a lifespan of around 12 years.

Breed 7

Bulldog

Bulldogs were originally bred for their courage and tenacity.

This iconic British breed has many loyal fans. The Bulldog is a member of the Utility group of dogs, and his wide, squat body and big broad head, with its jutting lower jaw, sets him apart from all other breeds. His distinctive features lend themselves to caricature and the use of the Bulldog by the media is widespread.

Bulldog registrations have increased steadily over the last decade, and now stand at just under 7,000 births a year. Not quite the meteoric rise of his French cousins, but this is a breed that is still growing in popularity. With a lifespan of just six to eight years the Bulldog is not in great shape. We'll look at why this is in the health section below.

Origins

The history of the Bulldog goes back a long way. Bulldog breeds were originally bred for their fierce courage and tenacity and for their power and their grip. They were used for the sport of bull-baiting, which was outlawed in 1835 through animal welfare legislation, and were probably used for farm work (controlling and guarding livestock) too. Some claim that Bulldogs were crossed with Pugs at some point to bring them down in size and flatten the face. When dog fighting took over as the gambling man's entertainment, Bull Terriers were favoured for their fighting spirit and Bulldog numbers declined. In the mid-1860s a small number of enthusiasts got together to rescue the breed and a temporary club was formed. The Bulldog Club proper was formed in 1875, and claims to be the first of the modern dog clubs as we know them today.

As the role of the Bulldog shifted to that of companion, the aggression was bred out of the breed. The breed has changed in other ways, too. Modern Bulldogs are a more 'squat' breed than the leggier ancestors we see in old paintings, and as skulls in the Natural History Museum of Bern show us, the Bulldog's skull has become increasingly shortened as the decades have passed by.

Breed characteristics

This is a smooth-coated, thick-set dog with a wide chest, large head and distinctive projecting and upturned lower jaw. The Kennel Club describes him as 'fierce in appearance but possessed of an affectionate nature'. The Bulldog has distinctive 'rose' ears which fold inwards and back, and the loose skin under his throat completes the look we all know so well. The Kennel Club specifies a weight of 25 and 22.5kg (55 and 50lb) respectively for males and females. His hindquarters should be high and strong, and his body well muscled. No height is specified, but a Bulldog will not usually be more than about 40.5cm (16in) at the shoulder. The KC allows the smooth coat in a number of different colours, including fawns, brindles and reds, and with or without a darker mask. Pied (white with another permitted colour) is also allowed. Black or black-and-tan is frowned upon.

Despite his ancestry, the Bulldog is not an aggressive breed, and would make a nice family companion were it not for his health problems.

Health and available screening tests

Many of the health problems suffered by the Bulldog are a direct result of the body shape we have given him. His extreme brachycephaly (short skull) interferes with his ability to oxygenate and cool himself, and raises the risk of eye problems. These issues are explained in detail in Chapter 4 – it's important that you read them, even if you have already decided to get a Bulldog, as they will help you prepare and care for your puppy.

In a recent study on the impact of facial conformation on canine health, 63 per cent of Bulldogs attending a clinic for routine appointments were found to have brachycephalic obstructive airway syndrome (BOAS). The study showed that there is a direct relationship between decreasing muzzle length and increase in respiratory problems. In addition to breathing and cooling difficulties, gagging, regurgitation, vomiting, dental problems and a range of eye conditions are also associated with brachycephaly. According to Petplan, the most common eye problem in Bulldogs is a condition called cherry eye –where the tear-producing gland pops out and sits on the surface of the corner of the eye.

Like all dogs with skinfolds, folds are susceptible to infection, and Petplan reports that skin conditions are the most common problem for which Bulldogs receive veterinary treatment. Bulldogs with screw tails can suffer from ingrowing tails. Their large heads and wide shoulders also lead to birthing difficulties, and most Bulldog puppies are born by caesarean section. Heart problems are another issue in the breed and are the leading cause of death in Bulldogs recorded in the Kennel Club's 2014 health survey. Bulldogs are also susceptible to hyperuricosuria (HUU), an inherited disease that predisposes the dog to painful bladder stones. There is a DNA test available for this condition.

Health statistics

The median age at death for the Bulldog recorded in the 2004 health survey is 6.9 years, a worryingly short life for a medium-sized dog. The 2013 study puts the median age at death as 8.4 years, though it is the smallest sample (26 dogs). The latest Kennel Club survey from 2014, which looked at 39 deaths, supports the lower figure and puts the Bulldog lifespan at 6 years.

Cancer rates are low – 18 per cent – however, cancer tends to attack older dogs and it would appear that, sadly, most Bulldogs don't reach old age.

Average coefficient of inbreeding: 10 per cent. The adverse effects of inbreeding become evident when the COI of a mating exceeds 5 per cent and it is a good idea to seek out a litter with a lower COI than this.

The Bulldog is listed as a category 3 breed by the Kennel Club under its Breed Watch scheme. Category 3 is for breeds where some dogs have visible conditions or exaggerations that can cause pain or discomfort. These are the point of concern for the breed as listed by the Kennel Club:

- Excessive amounts of loose facial skin with conformational defects of the upper and/or lower eyelids, so that the eyelid margins are not in normal contact with the eye when the dog is in its natural pose
- Hair loss or scarring from previous dermatitis
- Heavy over-nose wrinkle (roll)
- Inverted tail
- Lack of tail
- Pinched nostrils
- Significantly overweight
- Sore eyes due to damage or poor eyelid conformation
- Tight tail
- Unsound movement.

These points are intended to guide judges at shows and to help them look for evidence that the dog has, or has had, one of the problems causing concern. A new health scheme for Bulldogs has recently been introduced to try and address some of these problems. There are, or will be, certificates at three levels: bronze, silver and gold.

Kennel Club recommended tests

The Kennel Club recommend the following schemes for the Bulldog:

- Breed Council – health certificate for breeding stock
- DNA test – HUU.

Health summary

Sadly, while not endangered, this is a breed that is currently in very poor health. If you buy a Bulldog puppy you need to be aware that his life may be relatively short and uncomfortable. Bulldogs can be difficult or expensive to insure due to their medical problems – I approached five insurance companies and two refused to quote for this breed.

General care

Despite his short, easy-care coat, the Bulldog does need a very thorough daily grooming routine. The skinfolds on a Bulldog's face and the area around his tail need careful daily cleaning and drying or they will become smelly and infected. You'll need to seek veterinary attention if your cleaning efforts are insufficient. Bulldogs with screw tails need extra care and many Bulldogs cannot reach their own bottoms, so keeping this area clean is down to you. You'll also need to clean your Bulldog's teeth daily, as overcrowded teeth are very vulnerable to infection and decay.

Exercise is an essential part of keeping any dog fit, but with Bulldogs there are some important safety issues that you must consider. The first is safety around water. Most Bulldogs cannot swim and those that can often don't swim well. Bulldogs can drown in quite shallow water and must never be left unsupervised near pools, ponds, rivers, etc. The second issue you need to consider is keeping your Bulldog's oxygen levels up. He cannot oxygenate himself efficiently and his airway can be compromised by even quite gentle exercise. This is why many Bulldogs are reluctant to race around for long periods of time and why those that do are susceptible to collapse. Bulldogs cannot easily cool themselves – even when panting heavily – so must not be subjected to high temperatures or exercised in warm weather. If you decide to buy a Bulldog puppy you need to be aware of the symptoms of respiratory distress in such dogs because this is a major risk to his health.

Leavitt Bulldogs are bred with health as a priority.

Final thoughts

- The Bulldog is truly a British icon and many people would love to own one. Most of those who buy a Bulldog puppy are simply unaware of the challenges facing this much-loved breed. This is a dog with a short lifespan and significant chance of ill health, chronic discomfort and the high medical insurance costs for this breed reflect the chances of a Bulldog needing major surgery during his lifetime.
- So many people are deeply concerned about the welfare of this English breed that a number of enthusiasts have set about breeding a healthier, better-constructed Bulldog. These 'new' lines of Bulldog are usually the result of outcrossing and are not recognised by the Kennel Club at the present time. Some of them are, however, an improvement health-wise and worth considering. One of these is the Leavitt Bulldog, and breeders can be found through the Leavitt Bulldog Association. Another alternative for those who want a sturdy medium-sized dog with a broad head and Kennel Club registration is the Staffordshire Bull Terrier.

Breed 8

Golden Retriever

The Golden Retriever descends from the Flat Coated Retriever. He has an interesting history and a fair dash of Spaniel blood in his veins. Originally a working Retriever, the breed is now divided into show and working lines, with show-strain dogs making up the vast majority.

There are around 7,000 Golden Retrievers born in the UK each year. This has fallen a little over the last few years, but that fall is in proportion to the overall fall in pedigree dog registrations, so the breed is fairly stable in terms of popularity. Like his Flat Coated predecessor, the Golden Retriever has a tendency to higher-than-average rates of cancer, so we'll be looking at what you can do about this if you are attracted to the breed. This is a well-constructed dog, renowned for his superb temperament, with a lifespan of some 12 years.

Golden Retrievers are fit, active, intelligent dogs.

Origins

The beginnings of the Golden Retriever breed are quite well recorded. At some point in the late 1800s, Lord Tweedmouth, an aristocrat from the Scottish Borders, bred a yellow Flat Coated Retriever with a Tweed Water Spaniel (now extinct).

He established the breed from the offspring of this litter, and is said to have used a number of other outcrosses in the process, including the Irish Setter. In 1908 some examples of the breed were exhibited in a Kennel Club show by Lord Harcourt and caught the public eye. The

Golden Retriever Club was formed in 1911. At this point the dogs were still classified as Flat Coated Retrievers, and were not registered as a separate breed until 1913.

The Golden Retriever was developed as a breed for retrieving in and around water. My very first Gundog, born in the 1960s, was a dual purpose Golden Retriever from the then famous Sharland Kennels in England. He was a family pet, but his father was a full champion (champion in the field and on the bench). Nowadays the lines are split and if you want a working Golden you need to go to a working Golden breeder. However, the vast majority of Golden Retrievers are much-loved family pets and as service dogs best known for their part in the Guide Dogs For The Blind breeding programme in the UK, where many guide dogs are first crosses between a Labrador and a Golden Retriever.

Breed characteristics

The Kennel Club describes the Golden Retriever as a powerful dog with a kindly expression and a balanced, well-chiselled skull. The recommended height for a Golden Retriever is 56–61cm (22–24in), females may be 5cm less, and weigh up to 36kg (80lb). Working-line dogs tend to be a little smaller than their show-bred cousins.

Because of his origins as a water dog, the Golden Retriever has a dense oily coat with a typical Gundog odour, especially when wet. His coat is medium length, and softly feathered with a water-resistant undercoat. The KC permits any shade of gold or cream, though lighter colours are currently more fashionable in the show ring.

The two strains of Golden Retriever that we see today are quite different in appearance. The Golden Retrievers of my childhood varied in colour from a rich dark russet to a warm golden colour. Working-strain Goldens still look like this, but during the last few decades the show strains of the breed have become much paler in colour with a more profuse coat. Working lines of Golden Retrievers are not that common and take some looking for, but are well worth the search, especially if the rich colours of yesteryear appeal to you. This is a shedding breed so expect a certain amount of hair in your home.

The Golden Retriever loves nothing more than to carry something around in his mouth, and will enjoy learning to fetch a ball or toy for you. Most love to swim and get muddy, and will keep up with a family hike from dawn till dusk. Golden Retrievers can be mouthy and determined chewers as puppies.

Most Golden Retrievers are pretty poor guard dogs and will welcome visitors, indiscriminately, into your home. Obviously, dogs with poor temperaments

Golden Retrievers come in a range of shades.

do exist in all breeds, but in most well-bred lines Golden Retrievers are kind, friendly dogs, boisterous when young, and with a happy, outgoing disposition. It is a testament to their intelligence and co-operative nature that Goldens are now widely used as assistance dogs.

Health and available screening tests

The most common health condition needing treatment in Golden Retrievers is joint trouble (Petplan). Goldens suffer from hip and elbow dysplasia, and there are screening programmes to help you avoid these. They are also prone to cruciate ligament problems. I referred earlier to cancer, and the incidence of this disease in Golden Retrievers is worryingly high. Petplan notes that lumps and bumps of all kinds are the second most common condition that they see in the breed. An important study has shown that the incidence of both cancer *and* joint problems is lower in Golden Retrievers that have not been neutered.

Health statistics

The median age at death of the Golden Retriever in the 2004 health survey is recorded at 12.25. This is supported by the 2013 study and by the Kennel Club's 2014 health survey.

According to the 2004 health survey close to 40 per cent of Golden Retrievers will die from cancer, compared with a cancer rate of 27 per cent in the general pedigree dog population. The American Kennel Club put the risk in the USA much higher at 57 per cent of females and 66 per cent of males.

Average coefficient of inbreeding: 9.4 per cent. The adverse effects of inbreeding become evident when the COI of a mating exceeds 5 per cent and it is a good idea to seek out a litter with a lower COI than this.

Breed median hip score: 10. The parents of your puppy should ideally be at, or below, this.

Kennel Club recommended tests

- BVA/KC Hip Dysplasia Scheme
- BVA/KC/ISDS Eye Scheme
- BVA/KC/Elbow Dysplasia Scheme
- Progressive Retinal Atrophy (GR-PRA1)
- Progressive Retinal Atrophy (GR-PRA2)
- DNA test – ICT-A.

Health summary

The Golden Retriever is a well-constructed dog breed with health tests available for the more common inherited conditions. Cancer is a problem in the breed, but you may be able to reduce this risk somewhat if you don't neuter your pet.

General care

This is an athletic, intelligent breed that needs an hour-and-a-half or more of exercise each day and thorough training. Fortunately, the Golden Retriever is generally a co-operative dog that is interested in interacting with people and easy to train. And he is happy to be outdoors in all weathers.

This is a breed with plenty of hair, some of which will find its way on to your furniture and clothes. All Golden Retrievers benefit from daily brushing, with particular attention paid to chest hair and 'trousers'. This will also help to minimise shedding. Some Goldens will need regular nail trimming depending on where they are exercised. If you don't like brushing dogs, this may not be the breed for you.

Final thoughts

- Perhaps the greatest attribute of the Golden Retriever is his outstanding temperament. He is good with children, but this is not a dog that is likely to guard your home, so don't expect him to bark at intruders. Golden Retrievers are great at tracking and finding things, and are easy to train. Many excel in obedience training and those from working lines can excel in the shooting field.
- Because of the cancer issues in the breed, and the belief that there is a genetic element to this, looking for lines with longevity is important. If you can pick a puppy with older parents, this may help to increase your puppy's chance of living a long life. Stud dogs can be used in matings up to and even beyond the end of the first decade, so this is something to take into consideration. Bearing in mind the cancer risk, you might also want to consider delaying or avoid desexing your dog. If you know you will need to neuter your dog, you might want to consider a less cancer-prone breed.
- A list of breed clubs for Golden Retrievers can be found on the Kennel Club website or from the Golden Retriever Breed Council. Although there are fewer of these than show-line or pet breeders, working lines are not that difficult to find via the Field Trial Secretary of your nearest Golden Retriever Club. Pet or show-bred Goldens will suit most families just as well, and are widely available throughout the UK. This is a dog you can have a lot of fun with, at home, in the park or on the beach; great with children and ideal for an active young family.

Breed 9

Border Terrier

The Border Terrier is a squarely built little dog with a coarse wiry coat in lovely earthy colours, a characterful whiskery face and an even temperament. There are 5–6,000 Border Terrier births in the UK each year, which makes the Border Terrier our most popular member of the Terrier group. However, like most of our Terrier breeds, the Border Terrier's popularity has slipped considerably over the last decade, probably due to the increase in interest in flat-faced breeds. This is a well-proportioned dog with a compact body, balanced skeleton, normal skull, plenty of stamina for an active life and a good lifespan of 12–14 years.

Border Terriers can make charming and fun family pets.

Origins

Many of our Terrier breeds are named after districts or counties, and, as his name suggests, the Border Terrier originates from the Scottish Borders. He was originally known under various other names also related to locations in that area – the Coquetdale Terrier is one, and the Redesdale Terrier is another. Paintings of dogs resembling Border Terriers can be found as far back as the seventeenth century. The breed we see today is claimed to be a composite of several other terrier breeds, including Bedlington Terriers (a long-legged Terrier breed) and the Dandie Dinmont.

The Border Terrier was recognised as a breed by the Kennel Club in 1920 and the Border Terrier Club was formed that same year. This was a working Terrier, used in fox hunting and expected to go to ground to bolt foxes from their lairs. He has longer legs than some of our modern working Terriers, and this is because the Border Terrier was also expected to keep up with the hounds and their mounted hunt followers. So, he needed to be small enough to fit down a fox earth and to have long enough legs to carry him long distances when necessary. You can still find Border Terriers at work in the countryside, but the vast majority of these little dogs are now family pets.

The Border Terrier is a healthy, active little dog.

Breed characteristics

The Border Terrier has a pretty, otter-shaped head with a short muzzle and dark eyes, framed by small ears tipped over and facing forwards. The Kennel Club describes a 'deep, narrow dog' and points out that like any Terrier he should be capable of being spanned by both hands behind the shoulder. The KC stipulates a weight for the Border Terrier of 6–7kg (13–15.5lb) for dogs and 5–6.5kg (11.5–14lb) for bitches. No height requirement is given, but the American Kennel Club describes the Border Terriers' proportions: 'the height at the withers is slightly greater than the distance from the withers to the tail, i.e. by possibly 1–1.5 inches [2.5–4cm] in a 14 pound [6.3kg] dog.' The Border Terrier's coarse, weather-resistant coat comes in a range of colours, including wheaten, grizzle-and-tan, red, and blue-and-tan.

Like most working Terriers, Borders are expected to be easy to handle and are generally even-tempered. It takes courage to go to ground against a predator, so like all Terriers bred essentially for fox control, Border Terriers are brave little dogs but while not slow to defend themselves if pushed around by other dogs, they are friendly and affectionate towards people. The Kennel Club terms this characteristic 'gameness' – an old-fashioned but nonetheless descriptive term. The Border Terrier is intended to be cheerful and friendly, but like all breeds this will depend to some extent on the way he has been bred and socialised. Like most Terriers he is not averse to barking and digging, and needs to be encouraged not to make a noise, or chase your other pets.

Health and available screening tests

In common with other small breeds patellar luxation (kneecaps popping out of joints) can be a problem in some Border Terriers. Skin allergies and ear problems may also occur. Canine epileptoid cramping syndrome (CECS) is a recently recognised inherited condition in the Border Terrier breed. It's a neurological condition causing episodes of cramping that involves the muscles and the intestines. The effects can vary from mild to severe, and the dog remains conscious throughout. It may be caused by a single gene and, if so, there is hope of a test being developed in the future. In some cases, the condition improves in response to changes in diet.

Health statistics

The 2004 health survey puts median age of death at 14 years, and this figure should be fairly reliable as there were over 150 dogs in the data sample. The KC's more recent survey with a smaller sample of Border Terrier deaths (98) showed a median age of death as 12 years.

This is a low-risk breed for cancer. Despite living to a good age, only 19 per cent of Border Terriers died from the disease.

Average coefficient of inbreeding: 8.8 per cent. The adverse effects of inbreeding become evident when the COI of a mating exceeds 5 per cent and it is a good idea to seek out a litter with a lower COI than this.

Kennel Club recommended tests

There are no screening tests recommended by the Kennel Club.

Health summary

A generally healthy breed with a good lifespan.

General care

Even small dogs need plenty of exercise. The Border Terrier is very adaptable and some of his daily exercise can take the form of games such as fetch or tug (most Terriers love playing tug), but it all needs to add up to an hour or so of vigorous exercise a day. The Border Terrier can and should be obedience trained, and will also enjoy all manner of activities, and outdoor expeditions in all weathers. This is a relatively easy dog to keep clean and smart. Although his coat is short, it sheds and does benefit from twice-weekly grooming.

Final thoughts

A little dog with a big heart, the Border Terrier is one of our most popular breeds for good reason. Although he is one of the smaller dogs in this section, the Border Terrier is no lapdog and will keep up with an active family. This is a healthy pet for a family looking for a small dog that will enjoy accompanying them on walks. His beds/crates don't take up much space, he doesn't take a lot of grooming, he won't eat you out of house and home, and with luck should be a part of your family for 12 to 14 years.

Breed 10

Miniature Schnauzer

The Miniature Schnauzer has a great reputation as a kind-tempered breed.

The Miniature Schnauzer is a sturdy little dog with a thick coarse coat. His whiskery face and beard give him added appeal and character, and in dogs being exhibited in the show ring this feature is accentuated by the way he is clipped and groomed. A member of the Utility group, he is the tenth most popular dog in the UK.

While many breeds are in decline, the Miniature Schnauzer has remained consistently popular for the last decade, with over 5,000 puppies registered each year in the UK, almost 1,000 more than a decade ago. A well-structured and fairly healthy breed of dog, the Miniature Schnauzer has a lifespan of ten to 12 years, with some individuals living well into their teens.

Origins

Schnauzers originally came from Germany. Enthusiasts claim that they may be recognisable from paintings as far back as the fifteenth century. They originally belonged to a group of German dogs known as Pinschers (a Terrier-type dog) – the Schnauzer name was adopted for the wire-haired version of this group, and the Bavarian Schnauzer Club formed in 1901.

The Miniature Schnauzer is a descendant of the standard Schnauzer, and the Miniature Schnauzer Club was formed in 1953. In appearance he is just a scaled-down version of the bigger breed, which may have been the result of mixing Affenpinscher, and possibly Poodle, with the standard-sized dog.

In the past, these were general-purpose farm dogs bred for catching rats, helping with livestock, as well as being used to guard rural properties. Nowadays this Terrier-like dog is usually purchased solely as a companion, but will happily act as a watchdog and alert his family to visitors.

Breed characteristics

The Kennel Club describes the Miniature Schnauzer as a 'reliable and intelligent' companion dog, a 'sturdy and sinewy' little dog with a desirable height of 35.5cm (14in) for dogs and 33cm (13in) for bitches. Weight can vary from 4.5 to 9kg (10–20lb), with most weighing in at between 5.5 and 8kg (12 and 18lb), a little less for females. The Miniature Schnauzer's beard and the way he is groomed gives him that very distinctive Schnauzer look. His wiry coat is low-shedding and the Kennel Club lists the acceptable colours as pepper-and-salt, black,

Miniature Schnauzers are healthy, active dogs.

black-and-silver, and white. White is a somewhat controversial coat colour in the breed and is not considered acceptable in the show ring in some countries.

The Miniature Schnauzer is not an unfriendly dog, but he will act as a watchdog – he will alert you to intruders and won't welcome them until you do. He can be quite vocal, and may greet his owner with some noise as well as enthusiasm. With a Terrier-like confidence, this little dog gets along with other dogs too, though he is not averse to defending himself if picked on. This readiness to self-defence means he is not as tolerant as some other breeds, and might not always be an ideal pet for children not quite old enough to understand and respect a dog's boundaries. On balance, though, the Miniature Schnauzer Club's description of a dog that 'ensures he enjoys life to the full and is game for anything . . . an excellent family dog' is a good one.

Health and available screening tests

Both hereditary cataracts (HC) and progressive retinal atrophy (PRA) can affect the Miniature Schnauzer. You should make sure that your Schnauzer pup comes from parents that have been tested under the relevant schemes for HC and PRA – this involves an annual eye examination for all breeding stock. One particular type of cataract problem, congenital hereditary cataracts, can be detected in small puppies, so ask if the litter has been or is going to be inspected.

According to Petplan, Miniature Schnauzers are three times more likely than any other breed to need treatment for liver disease. Pancreatitis is the fourth most common disease to affect them, and they are also more susceptible to diabetes than some other breeds.

Health statistics

According to the 2004 health survey of purebred dogs, the Miniature Schnauzer is recorded as having a median age at death of 12 years, with age at death in the Kennel Club 2014 health survey recorded at 10 years. The incidence of cancer is 21 per cent in the Miniature Schnauzer, well below the average for a dog.

Average coefficient of inbreeding: 5.1 per cent. The adverse effects of inbreeding become evident when the COI of a mating exceeds 5 per cent and it is a good idea to seek out a litter with a lower COI than this.

Kennel Club recommended tests

- BVA/KC/ISDS eye scheme.

Health summary

The Miniature Schnauzer is a relatively healthy breed. Make sure you buy from eye-tested stock and you should have a good chance of a healthy puppy.

General care

Half-an-hour's walk morning and evening, or the equivalent time spent playing ball games in an outdoor space, will keep this dog healthy and happy, though he'll be delighted to accompany you on much longer trips. Like all dogs, he needs regular training to make sure that he will come when called and walk nicely on a lead. He is an intelligent, alert little dog, quick and willing to learn, so this shouldn't cause you too many problems.

The Miniature Schnauzer is a low-shedding breed but the coat is not low-maintenance, and these are dogs that need regular grooming. Unless you are particularly handy with clippers and a comb, your Miniature Schnauzer will also benefit from regular trips to a professional groomer. Failure to groom your dog may result in a matted coat.

Final thoughts

- This is a breed that may well suit someone living in a town or without a great deal of space. But he'll be equally happy in the countryside, where he'll alert those living in rural properties to approaching visitors. He needs regular daily walks but you don't need to be a fitness fanatic to keep him happy.
- Because he doesn't shed much, the Miniature Schnauzer can make a suitable pet for someone with allergies. But if you know you are allergic, spend some time around other Miniature Schnauzers before you purchase your own, as there are no guarantees.
- The Miniature Schnauzer is an intelligent and relatively healthy Terrier-like dog, suitable for a family once children are past the toddler stage. You'll need to seek out eye-tested puppies, and your best bet for finding these is probably to find a breeder via a club in your region. With 5,000 pups born each year, you shouldn't find it too difficult to get a well-bred puppy in the UK. A good starting point would be a Miniature Schnauzer club. There are three in Great Britain alone, and you can find them on the Kennel Club website.

Breed 11

Staffordshire Bull Terrier

Sometimes mistaken for the larger Pit Bull Terrier, the Staffordshire Bull Terrier has the courage and tenacity of his working Terrier cousins but is altogether a more muscular and powerful dog, with a very short, smooth coat and rather blocky head.

Popularity of the Staffordshire Bull Terrier has declined steeply over the last decade, from over 12,000 puppy registrations a year down to less than 5,000. It is, however, still the second most popular member of the Terrier group in the UK. The rise and rise of the slightly smaller French Bulldog has undoubtedly been a factor in the Staffie's decline, but so too has an unenviable reputation for fighting and biting. We'll have a look at that in a moment.

Staffies might look tough, but they can make loving and loyal pets.

The muzzle on some Staffordshire Bull Terriers can be a little on the short side. Other than that, the Staffordshire Bull Terrier is a well-constructed, sturdy, trim dog and has a lifespan of 11 to 13 years.

Well-bred Staffies are fit, active and great fun.

⁂ Origins

This is a British breed created by mixing Bulldog and Terrier bloodlines to provide a powerful and brave dog that could be used to fight other dogs. The sport of dog fighting was developed to replace the bull-baiting and bear-baiting that was outlawed in Britain in 1835. One hundred years later, in May 1935, the Kennel Club recognised the Staffordshire Bull Terrier as a breed in his own right, and the Staffordshire Bull Terrier Club was formed that same year.

Despite their history, most Staffordshire Bull Terriers these days are much loved and affectionate family pets, but the breed has had a bad press, and some unpleasant news stories may have contributed to the recent drop in puppy sales. The Staffie's reputation, it should be said, is probably more a reflection of those who sometimes own them than a direct result of any aspect of this dog's temperament. These are dogs that have a 'tough' appearance, and that has made them attractive to those who wish to appear tough themselves. Sadly, when a dog is used in this way it is likely to be badly raised and poorly socialised, thus fulfilling the owner's desire for an aggressive and unpleasant animal. The well-bred Staffie, raised in a caring family, is a very different dog.

Breed characteristics

This is a small but powerful dog who reaches no more than 40.5cm (16in) at the shoulder. His broad chest, wide muzzle and chiselled face give him his tough appearance, while his small ears accentuate the breadth of his skull. Despite his small stature the Staffordshire Bull Terrier that can weigh from 12.5–17kg (28–38lb), females a little lighter. He's a veritable power pack that needs training to walk nicely on a lead if you don't want to be dragged around behind him. The Staffie's sleek coat comes in a wide range of colours: red, fawn, white, black or blue, any one of these colours with white, or any shade of brindle or any shade of brindle with white. Dogs that are black-and-tan or liver are considered undesirable and are not eligible to compete in the show ring. This is a shedding breed, but not excessively so.

This is not an aloof dog. A well-bred Staffie is a wriggling bundle of friendliness, delighted to meet and greet friends and strangers alike, gentle with children and endlessly enthusiastic for walks, games and fun. Like other Bull breeds, the Staffordshire Bull Terrier has the potential for a gripping bite and having bitten is inclined to 'hold on'. Fortunately, most Staffies will never bite anyone. On the contrary, the Kennel Club describes the Staffie as 'kindness itself'. Its breed standard describes the Staffordshire Bull Terrier as 'highly intelligent and affectionate, especially with children' and further describes the Staffie temperament as 'totally reliable'. While adoring people, especially children, some Staffies can be short on patience with other dogs and may chase cats or small animals if not raised carefully together. So this is a breed that needs some supervision outdoors.

Health and available screening tests

According to pet insurers Petplan, the issue most likely to send a Staffordshire Bull Terrier to the vet is skin problems, with lumps and bumps coming in second, and a higher-than-average rate of cancer in the breed. Petplan also note that Staffordshire Bull Terriers are twice as likely to suffer patellar luxation (kneecaps popping out of joint) as any other breed. Staffies suffer from hereditary cataracts (HC), which can affect puppies as young as nine months old, and if left untreated, progress to blindness in the still-young dog. They also suffer from a metabolic disorder called L-2-HGA that affects the nervous system, causing seizures, tremors and other problems. It usually manifests itself in puppies over six months old. There are tests available for these conditions – another reason for buying a Staffie from a responsible breeder.

Some Staffordshire Bull Terriers are slightly brachycephalic (short-skulled) and in a recent study on the impact of facial conformation on canine health, 6 per cent of Staffies attending a clinic for routine appointments were found to have some degree of brachycephalic obstructive airway syndrome (BOAS).

Health statistics

The median age of death for Staffordshire Bull Terriers is 12.75 years according to the 2004 health survey, 10.7 years according to the 2013 study and 11 years according to the KC 2014 survey.

The incidence of cancer appears to be high in Staffies at 44 per cent, so consider whether or not you will need to neuter your dog as this has been shown to *raise* the risk of cancer in a number of breeds.

Average coefficient of inbreeding: 7.6 per cent. The adverse effects of inbreeding become evident when the COI of a mating exceeds 5 per cent and it is a good idea to seek out a litter with a lower COI than this.

Kennel Club recommended tests

The Kennel Club recommend that Staffordshire Bull Terriers used for breeding have the following health clearances:

- BVA/KC/ISDS Eye Scheme
- DNA test – HC-HSF4
- DNA test – L-2-HGA.

And it suggests litter screening for PHPV.

Health summary

This is a moderately healthy breed with a largely sound body structure, though some individuals may be a little short in the muzzle for optimum health.

General care

This is a lively dog that needs to be exercised daily for an hour or so, and may be very happy to go further. He doesn't need a huge garden, and most Staffies will adjust well to apartment life if regularly exercised outdoors. Care needs to be taken in hot weather, as some Staffies are not great at keeping themselves cool and can be prone to heatstroke.

Although fairly small, the Staffordshire Bull Terrier is a strong dog and will benefit from regular daily training sessions to teach him to walk nicely on the lead. The Staffordshire Bull Terrier's coat is very low-maintenance, a quick once over with a body brush every few days, with some extra brushing during periods of shedding, will keep him shiny and dust-free.

Final thoughts

- This is a breed with a tarnish to his reputation that is largely undeserved. A well-bred, well-socialised Staffie makes a delightfully happy, friendly, easy-going and safe family pet. It is true that the breed is popular with people who may misuse the Staffie and so it is especially important to buy from a responsible breeder whose dogs can all be clearly seen to be unreservedly friendly and confident around visitors, and where temperament is of paramount importance. A well-known show breeder is a good place to start, and will help you to avoid the small element of Staffordshire Bull Terrier breeders that have created the dogs you read about in the newspapers.
- The Staffordshire Bull Terrier is best suited to a temperate climate as he can be prone to overheating, but can cope with a moderate amount of exercise and is an otherwise healthy, happy breed of dog.

Breed 12

Cavalier King Charles Spaniel

The Cavalier King Charles Spaniel is one of the largest members of the Toy group. A small Spaniel with a pretty face and gentle temperament, this is a breed that is currently causing a great deal of concern.

Although still the twelfth most popular breed in the UK, registered births of Cavaliers have plummeted in the last decade, from over 11,000 in 2006 to just over 4,000 in 2015. It is likely that public awareness of the health issues in this breed has been a significant factor in its decline. We'll discuss these health problems below. The Cavalier King Charles Spaniel has a lifespan of about ten years.

A Small Spaniel with a gentle temperament, the Cavalier breed faces a number of serious health problems.

Origins

To understand the history of the Cavalier King Charles Spaniel, we need to look at his predecessor, the smaller King Charles Spaniel, a Toy Spaniel of the type beloved of the monarch he is named for. An example can be seen in the 1637 painting *The Five Eldest Children of Charles I* by Anthony Van Dyck (the smaller dog), and similar red-and-white Toy Spaniels can be seen in paintings much earlier than this. With the rise in popularity of the Pug in the eighteenth century, flatter-faced dogs became more sought after and the King Charles Spaniel was bred to be increasingly brachycephalic (short-skulled).

The name King Charles Spaniel was officially allocated to various different Toy Spaniels in 1903, reportedly on the wishes of Edward VII. In 1926 an American, Roswell Eldridge, lamenting the loss of the 'long-nosed' Toy Spaniels found in seventeenth-century paintings, offered a prize for the 'old type' of Spaniel and as a result, a few enthusiasts then formed a new breed that would become the Cavalier King Charles Spaniel we know today. The breed is a larger and less brachycephalic version of the King Charles Spaniel. A club was formed for this new breed but the Kennel Club did not recognise the Cavalier until 1945.

Breed characteristics

The KeAel Club describes the Cavalier as an active and graceful dog with a gentle expression. This is a small Spaniel with a fairly long, silky coat and feathered legs. Unusually, the Kennel Club specifies a muzzle length for this breed, which it states should be 4cm (1.5in) from stop to nose tip. While the facial structure of the Cavalier is an improvement on the King Charles Spaniel, this is still a brachycephalic breed. The Cavalier weighs between 5.5 and 8kg (12 and 18lb) and measures 30–33cm (12–13in) tall. There are four recognised colours: solid black with tan markings, solid ruby (a deep, rich red colour), Blenheim (chestnut patches on a white background) or tricolour (black patches on a white background with tan markings).

The Cavalier is not a sporting Spaniel but a companion dog, and this has been the role of King Charles Spaniels for hundreds of years. The temperament of these dogs is ideal: friendly, openly affectionate and with no trace of aggression. The Cavalier King Charles Spaniel would be the perfect family pet were it not for the extensive health problems that beset the breed.

Health and available screening tests

The Cavalier King Charles Spaniel suffers from two very serious diseases: Syringomyelia (SM), and mitral valve disease (MVD). SM is a painful neurological condition found most often in brachycephalic Toy dogs. The symptoms begin with persistent neck scratching, even though there appears to be nothing irritating the dog's skin. It can progress to intractable, unbearable pain. There is no simple test, but breeding stock can be MRI-scanned for potential problems. The cause lies in the domed shape of the head, which allows insufficient space at the back for the brain.

MVD is the most common illness seen in this breed and causes premature ageing of the heart. A study of 394 Cavaliers found heart murmurs indicative of MVD in 22 per cent of all Cavaliers across the whole age range, but by ten years of age almost all the dogs in the study were affected. Many experts believe the disease is now so widespread that the breed can only be saved by outcrossing.

These two diseases are not all the Cavalier has to contend with. In the 2015 study on the impact of facial conformation on canine health, 4 per cent of Cavalier King Charles Spaniels were found to be suffering from brachycephalic airway obstructive syndrome (BOAS). And Cavaliers are prone to eye diseases including cataracts and multifocal retinal dysplasia. Pet insurers Petplan say that Cavaliers are twice as likely to need treatment for eye conditions as other dogs they insure. They are also susceptible to a neurological condition called episodic falling (EF), and to a painful and incurable condition affecting the eyes called dry eye syndrome. There are DNA tests available for the latter two conditions.

Health statistics

The 2004 health survey (682 deaths) recorded a median age at death of 11.38 years for Cavaliers, with the 2013 study and the 2014 study recording 9.9 and 10 years respectively. The latter two were smaller but substantial samples (124/223 deaths).

Average coefficient of inbreeding: 5.5 per cent. The adverse effects of inbreeding become evident when the COI of a mating exceeds 5 per cent and it is a good idea to seek out a litter with a lower COI than this.

Health testing is essential if you want to buy a Cavalier King Charles Spaniel.

Kennel Club recommended tests

Recommended schemes and tests are as follows:

- BVA/KC/ISDS Eye Scheme
- Breed Club – Heart testing (mitral valve dysplasia)
- BVA/CK CMSM Scheme
- DNA test – EF
- DNA test – CC/DE.

Only the Eye Scheme is mandatory for KC Assured Breeders.

Health summary

A breed with serious health issues, susceptible to painful and distressing diseases.

General care

Although well feathered, the Cavalier's coat is fairly manageable and you will probably get away with a good grooming once or twice a week. The Cavalier will be happy with an hour or so of daily exercise and part of that can be a ball game in the garden if you prefer. He isn't difficult to train and in good health, he'll walk for longer if you want him to.

Final thoughts

This is a charming, loveable and beautiful dog, excellent with children, and completely free from aggression. Sadly, the health of the breed is very poor, and for this reason I am unable to recommend the Cavalier King Charles Spaniel as a family pet. If you decide to go ahead and buy a Cavalier puppy it is important that you go to an experienced breeder who recognises the problems in the breed and has carried out all the relevant tests. It is also important to recognise that, even with these precautions, there are still significant health risks for your dog. Only you can decide if you want to take this chance. If you decide to avoid the breed, some healthier small breed alternatives are the Miniature Poodle and the Border Terrier, or the slightly larger Cocker Spaniel.

Breed 13

Chihuahua

Chihuahuas can have a variety of lovely different coats.

The Chihuahua is a member of the Toy group of dogs. There are two Chihuahua breeds, long-coated and smooth-coated, and they are our smallest pedigree dogs. Often portrayed in the media as yappy lapdogs, the Chihuahua is actually a dog with a lot of personality. Ten years ago, the Chihuahua (Long Coat) was the most numerous of the two breeds, but the situation is now reversed and the Chihuahua (Smooth Coat) is now the more popular breed.

The Chihuahua is a brachycephalic (short-skulled) breed with a high-domed skull, but has sufficient length of muzzle to enable him to cool himself reasonably well. Popular with urban dwellers due to his diminutive size, his tiny body is reasonably well proportioned, but vulnerable to accidental injury. There are many claims for great longevity in the breed and some individuals do live to a ripe old age. The average lifespan, however, is probably not much more than 12 years.

Origins

While the name Chihuahua comes from the Mexican Town of Chihuahua, the origins of this little dog are disputed. Most sources refer to artefacts and artwork, in which Chihuahua-like dogs are represented, going as far back as ninth-century Mexico. The Kennel Club postulates that the Chihuahua may have originated in the Orient. Whoever is right, there have certainly been Chihuahuas as we know them today in Mexico since the mid-1800s and the breed was recognised by the American Kennel Club in 1904. There are claims that the Aztecs raised little dogs like these for food, or that they may be descended from companion dogs owned by the Toltec people. We don't really know. What we do know is that they have become a popular companion dog today, especially for apartment dwellers and those living in city centres.

Breed characteristics

The Kennel Club describes the Chihuahua as 'small, dainty and compact'. It describes the distinctive 'apple dome' of the Chihuahua's head, which is a feature of show-bred Chihuahuas. A weight of up to 2.5kg (6lb) is suggested, with an ideal minimum weight of 2kg (4lb). You sometimes find smaller Chihuahuas than this, often referred to as teacup dogs. Unusually, any colour or mixture of colours is acceptable to the Kennel Club, with the exception of merle. Protruding eyes are considered a fault, though this is a common problem in the breed due to the structure of the skull.

Chihuahuas have something of a reputation for being aggressive and snappy. This is probably partly related to the way they are raised and treated. Often treated as 'indoor only' dogs, it is likely that a substantial proportion of Chihuahuas are inadequately socialised as puppies. The American Kennel Club describes the Chihuahua as having Terrier-like qualities. A study in 2008 showed that Chihuahuas were one of two breeds most likely to be aggressive towards people – the other breed was the Dachshund. Many Chihuahua fans describe these little dogs as 'feisty'. That being said, aggression is unacceptable in any companion dog and temperament is something you do need to prioritise when you are choosing a Chihuahua puppy.

Health and available screening tests

The Chihuahua is often described as generally healthy. Most of the problems he does have are due to his tiny size and the shape of his head. This is also a breed that is at risk from injury, both from being carelessly handled and from being roughly treated by larger dogs. Chihuahuas are born with an open fontanelle or soft spot in their skull. The fontanelle may close as the Chihuahua grows and matures, but sometimes it remains open and is another point of vulnerability.

Patellar luxation (kneecaps popping out of joints) is a problem in Chihuahuas; according to a recent study, the Chihuahua is one of the three breeds most likely to suffer from this condition, especially if individuals are particularly small, female or neutered. Chihuahuas are also prone to Legg-Calve-Perthes disease (LCPD), which causes damage to the hip joint and for which treatment may require surgical intervention.

Heart problems and tracheal collapse are problems that can occur in the breed. Pet insurers Petplan say that Chihuahuas are twice as likely to need treatment for a heart condition as the other dogs they insure. They also note tracheal collapse as a breed problem for which surgery may be required. Low blood sugar and dental problems are common in very small dogs, and Chihuahuas are no exception.

Health statistics

Chihuahuas are reputedly very long-lived dogs, but while there is a potential for longevity in the breed, the evidence suggests it doesn't necessarily apply to the majority of these little dogs. The health survey from 2004 recorded a median age at death of 12.4 (71 deaths recorded), the 2013 study records a median age at death of just 7 years in the Chihuahua (out of 36 recorded deaths), but both studies recorded *some* individual dogs living up to almost 20 years.

Average coefficient of inbreeding: 5.8 per cent. The adverse effects of inbreeding become evident when the COI of a mating exceeds 5 per cent and it is a good idea to seek out a litter with a lower COI than this.

Kennel Club recommended tests

There are currently no Kennel Club recommended health tests for Chihuahuas used for breeding in the UK.

Health summary

This is perhaps best described as a moderately healthy and potentially long-lived dog, vulnerable to injury and prone to tracheal collapse and knee problems.

General care

Like many small dogs, Chihuahuas may feel the cold. They also need careful handling and to be protected from attacks by other dogs. Because they are so easily 'scooped up', many Chihuahua owners fail to train their dogs, but a good solid recall response can be a lifesaver. The Chihuahua is a clever dog, and not difficult to obedience train, though some owners report that house training requires a little more time and patience than with other dogs. All Chihuahuas should have their leash attached to a body harness, not a neck collar, as putting pressure on a collar may cause or exacerbate tracheal problems. Chihuahuas don't need very long walks but like all dogs will benefit from exercise and time spent outdoors.

Chihuahuas, like other tiny dogs, need smaller, more frequent meals than larger dog breeds. This helps them to keep their blood sugar levels stable and avoids hypoglycaemic attacks. Although his coat needs minimal attention, you'll need to clean your Chihuahua's teeth daily as his overcrowded teeth are very vulnerable to infection and decay.

Final thoughts

- The Kennel Club describes the Chihuahua as an ideal pet for the elderly. Families with young children are not usually suitable for Chihuahuas as these little dogs are easily injured through careless handling or dropping, and may have an uncertain temperament. If you decide on the Chihuahua as your choice of dog, make sure you see both parents and can confirm that they are friendly and good-natured.
- This is a breed with some health issues related to structure, though some individuals may live a very long time. There are seven Chihuahua breed clubs in the UK at the time of writing and they are a good place to begin when looking for one of these characterful and portable canines.

Breed 14

Shih Tzu

The Shi Tzu's coat requires thorough and regular grooming.

The Shih Tzu is a distinctive member of the Utility group of dogs. This is a small dog with long flowing hair, an even longer history and a big fan base. Always a companion dog and originally from the mountains of Tibet, the Shih Tzu has become enduringly popular. Shih Tzu registrations have fallen only slightly from just over to just under 4,000 births per year over the last decade. Bearing in mind the general fall in pedigree registrations, this is a breed that is holding its own. The friendlier of our two popular Tibetan breeds, the Shih Tzu has a high-maintenance coat and a lifespan of around 13 years.

Origins

The Shih Tzu is often thought of as being oriental in origin; its roots can be traced back to Tibet, where like the Lhasa Apso, the Shih Tzu was a prized member of noble households and monasteries. Unlike the Lhasa Apso, this breed was not expected to act as a sentinel. His purpose as primarily a companion, and even bed warmer, has created a dog with a softer temperament than his feisty cousins.

The Shih Tzu probably moved to China from Tibet in the 1600s and was developed there as a breed by the Chinese Empress Dowager Cixi. At some time during their history, the Shih Tzu bloodlines were most likely mixed with those of the Pug or Pekingese, and the breed is now somewhat flat-faced. Only a small number of dogs survived the Communist Revolution and a few individuals finally made it to Europe in the 1920s. The Shih Tzu grew steadily in popularity after Kennel Club recognition in the 1930s, and by 2012 had reached its current position as the fourteenth most popular breed in the UK.

Breed characteristics

Slightly longer than tall, this is a small and brachycephalic (short-skulled) dog. His dropped ears are moderately long and the Shih Tzu carries his tail over his back. He is a little taller than the superficially similar Lhasa Apso. The Kennel Club recommend a maximum height of 26.5cm (10.5in) and give a weight guide of 4.5–7.5kg (10–16lb).

The Shih Tzu is a supposedly non-shedding breed that some people with allergies may be able to tolerate. The fur on the Shih Tzu's face grows outwards from the centre, giving the breed the alternative name of Chrysanthemum Dog. The coat is thick, straight and very long – growing past the dog's feet if not kept well clipped. All colours are permissible, with particolours being especially popular when accompanied by a white blaze.

This is an affectionate and unreservedly friendly little dog – very different in temperament to the Lhasa Apso – and the Kennel Club describes him as 'bouncy and outgoing'. The Shih Tzu also has a tendency to bark.

Health and available screening tests

Shih Tzus have a number of health issues caused by their size and brachycephalic skull, and because they have chondrodystrophy – a type of dwarfism. They are prone to overheating and breathing difficulties as a result of brachycephalic obstructive airway syndrome (BOAS), and to spinal problems including intervertebral disk disease (IVDD). According to a study on the impact of facial conformation on BOAS, 8 per cent of Shih Tzus presenting at a veterinary

The Shih Tzu is a reasonably long-lived dog with a lower-than-avergae rate of cancer in the breed.

hospital for routine appointments were affected by this distressing condition. Unfortunately, both spinal and breathing difficulties can affect the dog at quite a young age. You can find out more information about these problems in Chapter 4.

In common with some other small dogs, the Shih Tzu's kneecaps are prone to pop out of joint (patellar luxation). According to pet insurers Petplan, Shih Tzus are most likely to need veterinary treatment for eye problems. Their protruding eyes are vulnerable to injury, and to painful conditions such as dry eye (where not enough tears are produced), corneal ulcers, entropion and distichiasis (where two rows of eyelashes rub the surface of the eye). Cherry eye (where the tear-producing gland pops out) can also be a problem in this breed. Shih Tzus are also predisposed to renal dysplasia, a kidney problem where the kidney fails to mature properly, and there is a screening test available for this. Small mouths come with dental problems and overcrowded and missing teeth are common. Skin allergies are the third most common health issue in the breed.

Health statistics

The 2004 health survey recorded a median age at death for Shih Tzus as 13.17 years (83 deaths recorded). The 2013 study also recorded a longevity of over 13 years, so it is probably safe to say this is a reasonably long-lived little dog.

The Shih Tzu has a lower-than-average rate of cancer at just 14.5 per cent of recorded deaths in the 2004 survey.

Average coefficient of inbreeding: 5.4 per cent. The adverse effects of inbreeding become evident when the COI of a mating exceeds 5 per cent and it is a good idea to seek out a litter with a lower COI than this.

Kennel Club recommended tests

There are no health tests recommended by the Kennel Club, but the following test is available to breeders:

- **Renal dysplasia (kidney disease).**

Health summary

This is a breed whose health is compromised by its structure and most health issues are related to its flattened face and spinal problems. Despite this, the Shih Tzu is a relatively long-lived dog and not prone to as many inherited diseases as some other breeds.

General care

This is not a breed with an easy-care coat. If you are going to let your Shih Tzu's coat grow to full-length you will need to be very committed to thorough daily grooming sessions. Most pet Shih Tzus are clipped fairly short. They still require some grooming but not on the same scale as a dog with a full coat. The short clip allows the dog freedom of movement and enables his owners to keep him clean. This is pretty much essential if you are going to take your Shih Tzu outside, and there are benefits to doing so. Fresh air and exercise is good for him and he needs to meet people in order to grow up confident and friendly. But be very careful around water. In common with other brachycephalic (short-skulled) breeds, the Shih Tzu is a poor swimmer and can easily drown. Small dogs benefit from frequent small meals rather than one big feed a day, and daily tooth brushing is essential in this breed to avoid periodontal (gum) disease, as overcrowded teeth trap food and cause infection and pain.

Final thoughts

- With minimal exercise requirements, the Shih Tzu is a breed that is capable of adapting happily to life in an apartment. This is an appealing little dog with a nice temperament, but his health is somewhat compromised by his structure. You must avoid overheating a Shih Tzu and be prepared for possible respiratory or eye problems. If you are looking for a small dog there are healthier alternatives such as the Border Terrier or Miniature Poodle.
- As with any brachycephalic breed, the longer the muzzle, the less the risk of the dog suffering from BOAS. This is something to bear in mind when looking at puppies and their parents.

Breed 15
Boxer

A fit and healthy Boxer will be an active member of the family.

The Boxer is a tall, muscular, short-coated dog, with plenty of energy and lots of enthusiasm. He is a medium to large breed with some guarding instincts, a distinctively marked coat and a wide, rather short skull. He is the most popular member of the Working group and is part of a wider group of dogs often known as Molossers. These are generally substantial, big-boned dogs with fairly heavy heads, who share a common ancestry.

The Working group has declined substantially in popularity over the last decade, and the Boxer is no exception, with registrations down to under 4,000 puppies a year compared with 9,000 a decade ago.

The Boxer would be a well-constructed dog were it not for the shortness of his muzzle, a feature that has become more exaggerated over time. Unfortunately, this handsome and popular breed is also prone to health troubles, and is not very long-lived. The lifespan of the boxer is around nine to ten years.

Origins

The origins of the Boxer lie in Germany. He is probably descended from the Bullenbeisser, a now extinct Mastiff-type breed, with some Bulldog bloodlines added in along the way. The Boxer was used for hunting and holding on to large prey, hence the strong athletic body and wide, gripping mouth with a set-back nose. There are many theories as to where the name 'Boxer' comes from, but it is likely to be derived from a German diminutive or nickname for one of the ancestors or local strains of the breed.

The Boxer Club was founded in 1896. The breed standard was set in 1902 and the Boxer was recognised by the American Kennel Club two years later. During the First World War, the Boxer was popular as a military service dog and only became more widely recognised as a family pet after the Second World War. The breed gained steadily in popularity worldwide, and is now the tenth most popular breed in the USA. Over time, the purpose of the breed has shifted from hunting partner to guard dog, and finally to the popular companion dog we know today.

Breed characteristics

This is a solidly constructed, squarely-built dog with a shortened skull (brachycephaly), some facial wrinkles and a wide mouth. His lower jaw is distinctively longer than his upper jaw, reflecting the Bulldog in his ancestry. The Boxer can reach up to 63.5cm (25in) tall and weigh up to 32kg (70lb), with females coming in at a couple of inches shorter and some 4.5kg (10lb) lighter. The Boxer has a short, easy-care coat that sheds, though not heavily. He comes in either fawn or brindle, and has a darker mask over his face, often overlaid with a white blaze and white muzzle patches. He may also have a white chest patch and white toes or socks. The Kennel Club states that no more than a third of the Boxer's body should be white.

Some exaggeration has crept into the breed in recent decades, with some lines of Boxer becoming increasingly brachycephalic and heavy-jowled. This is a problem for Boxers because brachycephaly comes with a range of health problems that increase in severity in proportion to the degree of skull shortening. A guarding breed, this is a confident dog who will act as watchdog and treat newcomers with some reserve. Affection is reserved for his friends, where it is given in abundance. Described by the Kennel Club as extrovert and energetic, the Boxer is certainly full of life. He's not aggressive, but nor does he allow other dogs to push him around.

Some Boxers are more brachycephalic than others.

Health and available screening tests

Boxers are susceptible to cancer and heart trouble. Mast cell tumours are the fifth most common illness in Boxers according to pet insurers Petplan, while cardiomyopathy is the most common heart disorder seen in the breed. The Boxer is prone to an inherited heart condition called aortic stenosis, which varies in severity and can be fatal. There is a screening programme that all responsible breeders participate in. As a moderately brachycephalic breed, Boxers are also prone to overheating. Some experts feel that show breeders of Boxers are selecting for increasingly short skulls and this is impacting on the fitness of these active dogs. Brachycephaly also increases the risk of eye problems in affected dogs and the most common eye problem that Boxers are treated for is corneal ulcers. A study looking at dogs attending the Royal Veterinary College Small Animal Referral Hospital for routine appointments during 2011 found that 18 per cent of Boxers suffered from brachycephalic obstructive airway syndrome (BOAS). A follow-up home study put this figure even higher at 50 per cent.

Another condition that is a cause for concern is seizures. Boxers seem to suffer more from primary epilepsy than other breeds and this tends to occur in quite young dogs. Research is underway to try and identify the gene, or genes, responsible. In common with many other larger breeds, Boxers are also prone to hip dysplasia and all breeding animals should be screened for this. Although not approved of by the Kennel Club, some Boxers are born white, and these dogs are prone to congenital deafness and may be more at risk from sunburn and associated skin cancers than other Boxers.

Health statistics

The 2004 pedigree health survey recorded a median age at death of 10.25 years for boxers; the 2013 study gave them 10 years and the 2014 KC study stated just nine years.

In the 2004 health survey 38.5 per cent of Boxer deaths were attributed to cancer. That is significantly higher than the 27 per centaverage for dogs.

Average coefficient of inbreeding: 7.1 per cent. The adverse effects of inbreeding become evident when the COI of a mating exceeds 5 per cent and it is a good idea to seek out a litter with a lower COI than this.

The median hip score for Boxers is 13. The parents of your puppy should ideally be at or below this.

Kennel Club recommended tests

- BVA/KC Hip Dysplasia Scheme
- Breed Club – Heart testing (aortic stenosis).

Health summary

The Boxer has quite a lot to contend with on the health front. Screening for heart and hip problems will help reduce the risks for you as a puppy buyer, as will selecting a puppy from lines with a less exaggerated degree of facial flattening. Boxers can be difficult or expensive to insure due to their medical problems – I approached five insurance companies and two refused to quote for this breed.

General care

Boxers are a brachycephalic breed, yet this is a dog that is expected to be active and even athletic. This can be a problem for Boxers, because some are sufficiently handicapped by their skull shape to be intolerant to exercise, especially in warm weather. If you live in a cool or temperate climate and your Boxer has sufficient length of muzzle you may be able to run or jog with him, but don't count on it. A good walk each morning and evening is a safer approach for this breed. And do make sure you know how to recognise and treat heatstroke. Many Boxers do better if kept out of direct sunlight and exercised in the cool of the day, for short periods of time.

The Boxer has a short, easy-care coat which sheds, though not excessively, and requires little more than a twice-weekly grooming with a body brush. As a guarding breed, you can expect your Boxer to let you know when strangers arrive at the house, and to take a little time to get to know new people. This is a large, intelligent dog that needs thorough socialisation and training in order to ensure he turns out to be a good canine citizen.

Final thoughts

- A healthy Boxer makes a great family pet, but finding one is not straightforward because the Boxer is not in terribly good shape right now. His skull shape compromises his health and comfort, cancer rates are on the high side, and he is prone to heart trouble. His lifespan could be better too. This ought to be a breed of dog that can live an active life and even go for a daily jog if that is your thing, but some breeders now warn against this because of the risk of overheating. Care needs to be taken when looking for a litter of Boxer puppies to avoid extremes of brachycephaly. It's worth studying a range of photos of the breed (as adults) to get a feel for the difference between longer- and shorter-skulled Boxers, so that you can choose more moderate parents for your puppy. There are 17 Boxer breed clubs in the UK, and you can find them on the Kennel Club website. To get a Boxer with a healthier length of muzzle you may need to cast your net further afield, making sure to check the health credentials of any litter carefully.

- There are other similar medium to large breeds in better health and with longer lifespans that you might want to consider. Other short-coated, energetic breeds you might like are dogs from the HPR subgroup of Gundogs – the Hungarian Vizsla (smooth coat) is a good alternative breed, as is the German Shorthaired Pointer.

Breed 16

Miniature Smooth-Haired Dachshund

The Dachshund is an instantly recognisable dog with his short legs and a long back. He was originally bred for hunting, and comes in six separate breeds, all genetically isolated from one another. We're mainly looking at the Miniature Smooth-Haired Dachshund here because this, the shortest member of our Hound group of dogs, is also the most popular.

Over 3,000 Miniature Smooth-Haired Dachshunds were registered with the Kennel Club in the year of writing (2016), and that number is almost double what it was ten years ago. This underlines the growing public preference for

Miniature Smooth-Haired Dachshunds are our most popular Hound breed.

smaller dogs. The Miniature Long-Haired Dachshund has declined in popularity, as Smooth-Haired numbers have increased. It is also interesting to note that the only small increase in full-sized Dachshund registrations has been the Wire-Haired variety. The Dachshund is a breed that has some temperament issues, and whose health is compromised by its extreme conformation, but with a lifespan of around 13 years.

Origins

Modern Dachshunds originate in Germany, and similar dogs have been found depicted in ancient artefacts. The word *dach* means badger and, as their name suggests, the Dachshund was originally bred for tracking and hunting badgers. Dachshunds were also used for fox and rabbit control and, reputedly, were once kept in packs for hunting larger game. The original dogs were smooth-haired, and a little longer on the leg than we see today – and therefore fitter and less prone to injury. It is claimed that the smaller Dachshunds were specifically bred down in size for rabbit hunting.

Opinions vary as to the breeds that were involved in the formation of this short-legged and feisty little dog, but may have included Pointers, Pinschers, Bloodhounds or Basset Hounds in varying combinations and proportions. It's possible that other breeds were brought in to create the different coat types, Spaniels for the long coat and perhaps wire-haired Pinschers or Pointers to create the wire hair. But it's all speculation and no one knows for sure.

Whatever their origins, Dachshunds go back several hundred years with a Smooth-Haired Dachshund clearly depicted in Jean-Baptiste Oudry's painting from 1740 of a *Hound with Gun and Dead Game*. This was a substantial dog probably weighing around 18kg (40lb), and modern Dachshunds have come down in size. The Dachshund arrived in Britain in the nineteenth century and became a favourite with Queen Victoria; the Dachshund Club was formed back in 1881. Like many German dogs, the two world wars dented the popularity of the breed, but they have recovered strongly to be one of our most popular pets. In the UK, a few Dachshunds are still used for hunting, Wire-Haired Dachshunds from working lines, known as teckels, are popular tracking dogs among the rural community, but, for the most part, modern Dachshunds are companion dogs.

Breed characteristics

Most people are familiar with the shape of the Dachshund, with his long, low-slung body and stumpy legs. Standard Dachshunds are quite substantial dogs and can weigh up to 12kg (26lb), whereas miniatures are much smaller. They weigh in at 4.5–5kg (10–11lb) and stand a mere 12.5–15cm (5–6in) tall. Miniature Smooth-Haired Dachshunds have very short, easy-care coats that shed moderately. They come in shades of red, black or chocolate. The black and chocolate varieties both have tan markings on eyebrows, socks and muzzle. Other colours are permitted, apart from white and dilutes. There is even a dappled variety, but pied and tricolours are considered undesirable.

The breed were originally tough, courageous little hunting dogs, and while most are now pets, they have retained their strength of character and are sometimes regarded as stubborn or difficult to train. A study published in 2008 showed that Dachshunds were among the two breeds most likely to show aggression to people (the other breed was Chihuahuas); this is something to consider when making your choice. Most Dachshunds will act as watchdogs and bark freely at intruders.

Health and available screening tests

There were data records from 296 Miniature Smooth-Haired Dachshunds in the 2014 pedigree health survey, and despite the median age of the group being only 3 years old, 30 of those dogs (10 per cent) had already been diagnosed with intervertebral disc disease (IVDD). Spinal disorders were also the leading cause of death in the breed. Although these spinal disorders aren't usually directly fatal, dogs that suffer from them may become paralysed or suffer intractable pain and may be euthanised to prevent further suffering. Interestingly, herniated vertebrae and IVDD were listed separately from spinal disorders in the survey,

Dachshunds also come in wire-haired and long-haired varieties.

but it is probably all the same to the dog. The Dachshund Breed Council have a graph on their health site showing that by 8 to 11 years of age, 30 per cent of Miniature Smooth-Haired Dachshunds have IVDD. Other studies have put this figure higher (see Chapter 4). The point for you is: this is not a rare condition, it is very painful for the dog and if you buy a Dachshund puppy, it is likely that your Dachshund will suffer from it.

The seriousness of the spinal issues in our Miniature Smooth-Haired Dachshund is obviously the overwhelming priority at the moment, but there are some other problems in the breed. In common with other short-legged dogs, Dachshunds are prone to patellar luxation (kneecaps popping out of joints). They are susceptible to progressive retinal atrophy (PRA), which causes blindness, and breeding animals must be tested for this condition. The Dachshund Breed Council have set up a helpful website focusing on Dachshund health issues (http://www.dachshundhealth.org.uk), where you can do further research and keep up with the latest developments on breed health.

Some Dachshunds come in an attractive dapple coat pattern. This pattern is also found in Border Collies and some other breeds, where it is known as 'merle'. The dapple or merle coat is caused by an abnormal gene, and this gene can be the source of some serious health problems. Unlike many of our inherited health problems, the dapple/merle gene is dominant – your puppy only needs one dapple gene to have the dappled coat pattern. However, when two dappled genes get together they can cause serious problems in some puppies (double dapple puppies can be blind, deaf or even born with no eyes, for example), while other puppies may seem to be unaffected. For this reason, double dapple is not accepted as a colour by the Kennel Club, and no responsible breeder will mate two dapple Dachshunds together and risk double dapple puppies.

Health statistics

The median age at death for Dachshunds (all breeds, 245 deaths recorded) in the 2004 health survey is recorded as 12.67 years. The 2013 survey recorded a longevity for Miniature Dachshunds in 2013 as 13.5 years. The Kennel Club's 2014 health survey recorded a median age at death of 6 years, but this was a sample size of only 19 recorded deaths.

Dachshunds have a low incidence of cancer at 16.7 per cent, compared with the 27 per cent average for dogs.

Average coefficient of inbreeding: 7.7 per cent. The adverse effects of inbreeding become evident when the COI of a mating exceeds 5 per cent and it is a good idea to seek out a litter with a lower COI than this.

The Dachshund is a category 2 breed on the Kennel Club's Breed Watch scheme, where the following points of concern are listed:

- **Bodyweight/condition.**

Kennel Club recommended tests

The only recommended test for the Miniature Smooth-Haired Dachshund is:

- **DNA test – PRA (cord1).**

The Dog Breed Health website recommends the following additional tests for Long- and Smooth-Haired Dachshunds:

- **Neuronal Ceroid Lipofuscinosis (degeneration of the nervous system).**

Health summary

Despite a reasonable lifespan this is a dog that has a significant chance of a painful and low-quality life from quite a young age. Larger Dachshund breeds may have a somewhat lower risk of spinal problems, but the only way to avoid these problems (and the suffering they cause) completely is to avoid buying a dog with this type of conformation.

General care

A short daily walk, 30 minutes or so, is sufficient for most Miniature Smooth-Haired Dachshunds, though some fitter dogs will enjoy more. It is very important that you protect your Dachshund's back, which is vulnerable to injury. Don't let him jump on and off the furniture, or out of cars. Lift him up and down from high surfaces when necessary; avoid them when possible. Dachshunds are intelligent dogs that can and should be trained. They also have excellent noses and may enjoy games and activities that involve tracking.

A Dachshund's coat doesn't need a huge amount of attention. Dachshunds do shed, though daily grooming will keep shed hair to a minimum.

Final thoughts

- This is a breed that can adapt to life in an apartment and doesn't need a great deal of exercise, but it is at risk of painful spinal problems. Miniature Dachshunds are quite vulnerable to injury if dropped or mishandled, and can be grumpy. They are therefore unsuited to families with small children. Even with careful handling, back problems are a distinct possibility. Due to the serious nature and prevalence of health issues in Miniature Short-Haired Dachshunds, this is not a breed I can recommend as a family pet. There are other small breeds, such as the Border Terrier, with longer legs that will stand a much better chance of a healthy, happy life.
- If your heart is set on a Dachshund, in the UK working Wire-Haired Dachshunds – teckels – tend to be higher on the leg and less exaggerated than show lines. If you decide to go ahead and purchase a Dachshund puppy, I recommend you choose the larger variety, and ensure that *both* the parents of your puppy are friendly and free from aggression.

Breed 17

Whippet

Whippets are fantastic sprinters, enjoying short but intense regular periods of exercise.

The Whippet is a sleek, narrow, slender, leggy little dog. He resembles a smaller version of the Greyhound and is designed to move with grace and speed. In the UK this is a breed with a devoted following, and Whippet numbers have remained fairly constant for the last decade. Around 3,000 Whippets are registered in the UK each year, making them the second most popular member of the UK's Hound group. They are popular pets and many Whippet owners enjoy competing in club races with their little sighthounds.

Free from exaggeration, the Whippet is a perfectly constructed athlete. It's a breed with a gentle temperament that currently enjoys excellent health, and has a lifespan of 12 to 13 years, with many individuals living longer.

Origins

The Whippet's origins lie in England. Sighthounds resembling Whippets and Greyhounds go back a long way, for instance in the 1725 painting *Misse and Turlu, Two Greyhounds Belonging to Louis XV* by Jean-Baptiste Oudry. It's likely that Whippets were bred down in size from larger Greyhounds to produce a useful ratting and rabbiting dog. According to the Whippet Club, back in the eighteenth century the word 'whippet' was simply used to denote any fast-running dog. Whippets were not only used to catch small animals, but also, for the amusement of their owners, were pitted against one another in races. Whippet racing became a highly popular sport in the mining communities of northern England.

The Whippet was recognised as an independent breed in the late nineteenth century, and the Whippet Club was formed in 1899. Whippet racing as a pastime is still enjoyed today by many enthusiasts, with events hosted by Whippet clubs on Sunday afternoons up and down the UK.

Breed characteristics

The original purpose of the breed was to outrun and catch small animals. The Whippet today is still capable of immense speed and has retained its athletic and healthy structure. Built like a miniature Greyhound, the Kennel Club describes a deep-chested dog with a broad muscular back and a definite 'tuck up', where the ribcage slopes steeply upwards to a tiny waist. Dogs should be 47–51cm (18.5–20in) tall, females a few centimetres shorter. Adult Whippets weigh around 11–13.5kg (25–30lb). The tail is long and tapering and the coat fine and close. Whippets do shed, but not excessively. The coat can be any colour or mixture of colours – soft blue greys and fawns, with or without white patches, are common.

Like all sighthounds, Whippets have a powerful chase instinct that is triggered by movement. Watching a fit Whippet accelerate to full speed in an open space can be breathtaking. However, these dogs are so fast and agile that the chance of them catching what they are chasing is very high. This means that Whippets need careful supervision and off-lead exercise and may need to be restricted to safe enclosures or remote areas where they cannot harm other people's pets. Despite their prey drive, these are quiet, gentle dogs, not usually demonstratively affectionate towards strangers, but never unfriendly or aggressive. Nervous individuals can occasionally be found and these should not be used for breeding.

Health and available screening tests

This is one of the shortest health sections in my breed reviews. Though in common with many pedigree breeds, the long-term future of pedigree Whippets is uncertain, Whippets as individuals are in pretty good shape. The Whippet Club claim that the breed is free from inherited diseases, and there are no health screening schemes or DNA tests recommended for the Whippet by the Kennel Club.

Health statistics

The 2004 pedigree heath survey gives the Whippet a longevity of 12.8 years (486 deaths recorded) and the Kennel Club 2014 survey with a smaller sample of 55 deaths

If you love spending time outdoors, a Whippet can make a fabulous companion.

found a median age at death of 10 years. There is quite a discrepancy here, but the larger sample is likely to be more accurate. The 2004 survey also states that the Whippet is one of the ten breeds most likely to die from old age.

Average coefficient of inbreeding: 9.5 per cent. The adverse effects of inbreeding become evident when the COI of a mating exceeds 5 per cent and it is a good idea to seek out a litter with a lower COI than this.

Kennel Club recommended tests

No tests or screening programmes are currently recommended by the Kennel Club for this breed.

Health summary

This is a soundly constructed, racing-type breed, where most individual dogs are in good general health. You stand a good chance of finding a puppy with a healthy future, though you should ideally try to find a litter from a mating with a lower than breed average coefficient of inbreeding.

General care

An easy breed to keep clean, the Whippet's fur coat needs minimal care and a rub with a damp cloth or sponge will remove most types of dirt or debris. Whippets have thin coats and minimal body fat, which means they can suffer from the cold and are better off living indoors in the warm. They certainly should not be kennelled in an unheated building during the winter months. In addition, when you exercise a Whippet outdoors in cold or wet weather he may need to wear a jacket or fleece to keep him comfortable.

Off-leash exercise needs to be supervised to avoid chasing disasters, but Whippets are not difficult to train. This is an athletic dog that needs an hour or so of daily exercise, including the opportunity to indulge his passion for running in a safe area. It is not always a breed that can be trusted around small pets, and unless raised with the family kitten, you may find it difficult to keep a cat and a Whippet together.

Whippets are ideally suited to a number of sports including racing, lure coursing, agility and flyball. Life with a Whippet should never be dull!

Final thoughts

There is very little that is negative about these elegant dogs. Some can be a little shy or hesitant, but a well-socialised puppy from confident parents will make a confident and happy family pet. Aggression is rare in the breed, and most Whippets are quiet, gentle, sweet-natured dogs that make entertaining and affectionate, if slightly bony, companions. There are 11 Whippet clubs and associations in the UK. They are a good starting point for finding a puppy and they can be found on the Kennel Club website.

Breed 18

Lhasa Apso

The Lhasa Apso is a little dog with a lot of character.

The Lhasa Apso is a small, long-haired dog belonging to the Utility group. This little dog was bred as a watchdog and has a tough character. Originally from Tibet, the breed has a long history, but is a relatively recent addition to the Kennel Club's portfolio of pedigree breeds. Less than 3,000 Lhasa Apso puppies are now registered annually, compared with over 5,000 just a few years ago. There are some health and temperament issues to consider, but this is a breed with a good lifespan of 13 to 14 years.

Origins

One of the oldest of our domesticated breeds, the origins of these dogs can be traced back thousands of years. The Lhasa Apso is named after the town of Lhasa in Tibet, and its roots probably lie in this mountainous region with its harsh climate. Lhasa Apsos were bred to act as watchdogs and to warn away intruders in monasteries and in the homes of Tibetan nobility. The Dalai Lama was said to have been involved with the management of the breed and would gift individual dogs or pairs of dogs to visiting dignitaries.

The Lhasa Apso arrived in Britain in 1920 and in the USA in 1925, it was temporarily classified as a Lhasa Terrier before being given its current name. This is a tough breed and the temperament of the Lhasa Apso reflects his original and important role as a sentinel. The Lhasa Apso's incredible long, thick coat was a protection against the harsh and inhospitable climate. Nowadays, the breed is regarded as more of a lapdog, but despite his small size and improvement in temperament in show lines, this is still a dog with attitude.

Breed characteristics

Somewhat longer in the body than his 25.5cm (10in) of height (females a little less), the Lhasa Apso is a small dog with a shortened muzzle relative to his head as a whole. The Kennel Club recommend a muzzle length for the breed of 4cm (1.5in), about a third of the length of the skull. The Lhasa Apso weighs in at between 6.5–8kg (14–18lb), females a little lighter.

This is considered to be a non-shedding breed. The coat is thick, straight and hard – it lacks the silky feel of many long-haired dogs. It can grow very long – so that it trails along the ground – and comes in a range of soft natural sandy golds and earthy blues, with attractive names like slate, smoke and grizzle.

The breed's original role has resulted in an independent dog with a strong guarding instinct and deep suspicion of strangers. Away from home, a Lhasa Apso should not be aggressive towards strangers who approach him, but to reach this point he needs to be subjected to some serious socialisation. While he is an excellent watchdog he isn't a yapper, and won't normally bark just for the sake of it.

Health and available screening tests

This is a moderately brachycephalic (short-skulled) breed with chondrodystrophy – a form of dwarfism. Although the Lhasa Apso is less severely brachycephalic than the more flat-faced Pug or Bulldog, for example, he is still prone to health problems associated with his conformation and small size. These include patellar luxation (kneecaps popping out of joints), intervertebral disk disease (IVDD), tracheal collapse and, most commonly, eye problems.

Like his close cousin the Shih Tzu, the Lhasa Apso is prone to a hereditary kidney problem called renal dysplasia, where the kidneys fail to mature properly.

Health statistics

The 2004 health survey recorded a median age at death of 14.33 years (out of 84 dogs); the 2013 study put the Lhasa Apso's longevity at 13 years.

The incidence of cancer in the breed is lower than average at 17.9 per cent.

Average coefficient of inbreeding: 11.1 per cent. The adverse effects of inbreeding become evident when the COI of a mating exceeds 5 per cent and it is a good idea to seek out a litter with a lower COI than this.

Kennel Club recommended tests

The Kennel Club recommend the following schemes for breeders of Lhasa Apsos:

- **BVA/KC/ISDS Eye Scheme.**

Health summary

A breed with not too many inherited diseases, the Lhasa Apso is somewhat compromised by its body structure and especially prone to eye and knee problems. Despite this, the breed, like many small dogs, is relatively long-lived.

General care

This is a breed that can get by on under an hour or so of exercise each day, but will walk further if you want them to. Like all courageous and independent breeds, getting involved in a battle of wills with a Lhasa Apso is a really bad idea. If you are going to get a Lhasa Apso puppy you need to be thoroughly familiar with positive, reward-based training methods, as these will get you the results you need to have a well-behaved and obedient dog.

This is a dog with a coat that takes a good deal of looking after. The Lhasa Apso is not suitable for anyone who doesn't enjoy wielding a brush! Keeping the coat clipped is essential if you want your dog to benefit from outdoor exercise. Clipping will cut down on the work involved and help to keep your dog comfortable. If you are going to let the coat grow, you will need to devote considerable time to grooming thoroughly every day.

Final thoughts

Because the coat doesn't shed much, the Lhasa Apso may be a suitable choice for *some* people with allergies. This is a breed that, given regular trips outdoors, will usually adapt well to apartment life, and will develop a strong attachment to his owner without being overly demonstrative. However, the temperament of these little dogs can cause problems for some owners. While affectionate with close family, the Lhasa Apso can be very suspicious of strangers. You'll need to work hard on socialisation to avoid aggression, and he isn't really an ideal pet for a family where young children often visit. Like many small popular breeds, Lhasa Apsos are frequently sold by commercial breeders (puppy farmers) and you need to be especially careful where you source your puppy. There are six Lhasa Apso clubs listed on the Kennel Club's website and this is a good place to begin your search.

West Highland White Terrier

The West Highland White is a distinctive Terrier that has changed little in appearance over the last hundred years or so. I have photos of my mother's pet Westie taken in the 1930s and she looks pretty much the same as the West Highland White Terriers you see today.

Currently our third most popular breed from the Terrier group, the West Highland White Terrier's popularity has fallen quite steeply over the last decade, from over 9,000 puppies registered in 2006 to under 3,000 in 2015. Despite declining numbers, this is a well-structured and long-lived breed. All three recent pedigree dog surveys agree on a lifespan of 13 years, and many Westies will live beyond this.

Westies have remained remarkably unchanged over the years.

Origins

The West Highland White's origins lie, of course, in the Highlands of Scotland, where hardy working Terriers with earthy red or wheaten coats have worked among the rocky cairns for hundreds of years. Darker-coated dogs were originally preferred, but it is said that the popular Cairn and other similar Terriers were prone to getting shot during vermin control activities, as they so closely resembled foxes in the undergrowth, and so white Terriers were bred in an attempt to make the Terrier stand out and protect him from accidental injury. Much of the credit for the development of the modern breed goes to the 16th Laird of Poltalloch, who in 1905 founded the West Highland White Terrier Club, which brought together his own white Poltalloch Terriers and other white Highland Terrier lines such as the Roseneath and Pittenweem Terriers.

The West Highland White Terrier was recognised by the Kennel Club in 1906 and by the American Kennel Club in 1908. While most Westies these days are bred as pets or for show, they have retained their physical attributes and sound construction, and are little changed from the white cairns of the past.

Breed characteristics

This is a compact little dog, just under 30cm (12in) in height. The West Highland White Terrier has a naturally short tail and distinctive upright ears. His dark eyes and nose are in sharp contrast to his white face. He weighs around 7.5–10kg (16–22lb), females a little less. He has a thick white double coat with a warm short undercoat and a longer harsh weatherproof outer layer which grows to about 5cm (2in) in length. The Westie does shed, but not excessively so. In show dogs the coat is often kept shorter on the neck and shoulders and left longer on the legs and belly. A fit, hardy dog with working origins, the modern Westie is usually kept as a pet, but will happily join in any outdoor adventures in any kind of weather. This is a friendly, fun dog, with all the typical confidence of a Terrier, and no trace of aggression.

Health and available screening tests

One of the most common problems in West Highland White Terriers is hypersensitive or itchy skin caused by allergies. Skin inflammation can be very distressing for a dog, but in many cases skin allergies can be treated and managed successfully.

Health statistics

The 2004 pedigree health survey recorded a median age at death of 13 years for the Westie and the 2013 and 2014 surveys supported this with 13.5 and 13 years respectively.

Average coefficient of inbreeding: 5.6 per cent. The adverse effects of inbreeding become evident when the COI of a mating exceeds 5 per cent and it is a good idea to seek out a litter with a lower COI than this.

The West Highland White Terrier is a category 2 breed under the Breed Watch scheme. Points of concern for judges are:

- **Misplaced lower canine teeth**
- **Skin irritation.**

Kennel Club recommended tests

No tests or screening programmes are currently recommended by the Kennel Club for this breed.

Health summary

This is a well-constructed little dog with no known structural defects. Skin troubles apart, the West Highland White Terrier is in relatively good health and has a reasonable lifespan for his size.

West Highland White Terriers are normally very healthy dogs.

General care

The West Highland White Terrier is a lively, outdoorsy dog who needs an hour or so of exercise each day. He will adjust to life in an apartment if taken out regularly, and if you are keen hiker your Westie will walk as far as you want to go. Like all Terriers, he is smart and determined. He needs regular training sessions to teach him to come when he is called. He can easily be taught to fetch a ball and will enjoy playing tug and getting involved in any family activities you can think up.

His coat needs a little bit of attention to keep it free from matts and tangles. A good grooming two or three times a week should be sufficient, and will minimise any shedding.

Final thoughts

- This is a playful, happy-go-lucky Terrier that makes a robust and enthusiastic family pet. Good with children, young and old, he stands a great chance of a long and healthy life. The breed is prone to skin problems and these can be inherited, so check that the parents of any litter you visit have not suffered from and are not being treated for any kind of allergy or itching.
- Show-bred Westies have not suffered from exaggeration, and there are seven breed clubs listed on the Kennel Club website. These are a good place to start your search for a West Highland White Terrier.

Breed 20

Beagle

With his upright tail and classic hound colouring, the Beagle looks a little like a smaller version of his Foxhound cousins. The Beagle's amazing sense of smell has proved useful in scent detection work and, in addition to having long been actively involved in hunting in the UK and beyond, he is also a popular companion dog.

With minor fluctuations, Beagle registrations have held steady in the UK at around 2,500 births a year since 2007, and this member of the Hound group is currently the fifth most popular dog in America. The Beagle is a relatively well-constructed dog, capable of achieving good levels of physical fitness and with a lifespan of 12 to 13 years.

Origins

Beagle-type scent hounds have existed for centuries. It isn't known exactly where they originated, but there are records from the eighth century of similar hounds. These include the St Hubert Hound that is an ancestor of the Talbot Hound, which in turn is an ancestor of the Beagle, having arrived in England from France in Norman times. Some have suggested that the word Beagle may have come from the French word *beugler* which means 'to bellow' – there's a hint in there! Another possible

Beagles are a fun-loving and playful breed.

derivation is the Celtic word *beag*, meaning small. Some fifteenth-century Beagles were actually tiny and were carried in hunters' saddlebags before being released to hunt under thick cover. This line of very small 'pocket' Beagles became extinct, and though some claim to have resurrected them, it is thought likely that these twenty-first-century pocket Beagles are miniaturised modern-day Beagles, rather than from the original bloodlines.

The modern Beagle was developed in the 1800s and probable ancestors include the Southern Hound (descended from the Talbot Hound), the North Country Beagle and the Harrier. In 1890 The Beagle Club was formed to promote the breeding of Beagles, and in 1891 the Association of Masters of Harriers and Beagles was formed to regulate the hunting activities of working Beagles. This is essentially a scent hound bred to hunt rabbits and hares, and intended to be followed on foot, rather than on horseback. Increasingly, however, the modern-day role of the Beagle is one of companion and family dog.

Even more popular as a pet in the USA than it is in Britain, the Beagle has been consistently in the top ten American Kennel Club registrations for decades.

Breed characteristics

The Beagle is a small compact hound, standing just 33–40.5cm (13-16in) tall. He is squarely constructed with legs and spine in proportion, and a typical upright Hound tail or stern. He resembles the Foxhound in colour and shape, but his face is distinctively Beagle. He has moderately long, fine ears, turned slightly forward to frame his face, and a white tip defines the end of his waving tail. He weighs 10–12.5kg (22–28lb) depending on his height; males can weigh a little more, females a little less. The Beagle's coat is short and weatherproof and comes in a range of traditional Hound colours, with patches of lemons, reds, tans, blues or black on a white background. The white is often confined to chest and lower legs with a splash on the muzzle and blaze on the forehead. The Beagle sheds his coat at intervals.

The Kennel Club describes the Beagle as 'amiable' and the Beagle is certainly a friendly though fairly independent dog. Hunting is his raison d'être, and all Beagles are happiest outdoors with their noses pressed to the ground. Like many Hounds, some Beagles do seem to enjoy the sound of their own voice, and will let you know if they are bored or have been left alone too long.

Health and available screening tests

Skin lumps and bumps are common in Beagles. Most of these are relatively harmless, but there is a higher-than-average incidence of cancer in the breed.

Musladin-Leuke Syndrome (MLS) is an inherited disease unique to Beagles. It interferes with the normal development of skin and other tissue and produces a dog with a distinctive tiptoe appearance and stiff gait. Neonatal cerebellar cortical degeneration (NCCD) is a progressive neurological disease that interferes with movement and balance. There is no cure, but NCCD is not usually an issue for puppy buyers because it affects very young puppies long before they are sold. There are DNA tests available for these conditions.

Health statistics

The median age at death for the Beagle is recorded as 12.67 years in the 2004 pedigree health survey (241 deaths) and 10 years in the smaller 2014 survey (36 deaths). The larger sample is likely to be a more accurate reflection of the Beagle's longevity.

The incidence of cancer in the breed is reported as 32.8 per cent – higher than the average of 27 per cent for dogs as a whole.

Average coefficient of inbreeding: 10.8 per cent. The adverse effects of inbreeding become evident when the COI of a mating exceeds 5 per cent and it is a good idea to seek out a litter with a lower COI than this.

Beagles were bred to hunt together in a pack.

Kennel Club recommended tests

The Kennel Club recommend the following tests or schemes:

- **DNA test – MLS**
- **DNA test – NCCD.**

The MLS test is compulsory for KC Assured Breeders.

- **Some breeders also test for IGS.**

Health summary

The Beagle is a well-structured dog. Buying from health-tested parents should ensure you get a puppy with a reasonable chance of a long and healthy life. Looking for a below-average coefficient of inbreeding is a good idea.

General care

The Beagle has a long history as an active working hound. He is capable of travelling long distances in a single day and can walk just as far as you are happy to go. He needs a minimum of an hour's daily exercise. This is not a clingy breed; your Beagle won't be hanging around your feet once you let him off the leash, and he will need to be specifically trained to come back when you call him. Hounds can be a little more challenging to train than Gundogs, for example, but it can and should be done.

The Beagle is a shedding breed, but other than twice-weekly brushing to remove dead hair his coat needs little attention.

Final thoughts

- A popular, fit, happy dog, the Beagle can make a great pet for an active family. He is sturdy, good with children and even-tempered. He'll enjoy joining in with family outings, and will happily accompany you on a daily jog.
- Beagle puppies should be chosen from health-tested parents. There are ten Beagle clubs and associations in the UK, and these are a good place to look for a Beagle puppy. A list of clubs can be found on the Kennel Club website.

Poodles, Doodles and Other Delights

We've looked at some of the most popular dog breeds in the UK today, but I couldn't leave you without talking briefly about some of the breeds which don't feature in our reviews. There are some wonderful dogs which didn't make it into the top 20 that I think deserve a mention. I'm going to finish this section with a quick look at Poodles, Poodle crosses, and few other breeds and crossbreeds, including some personal favourites of mine. Let's first look at which breeds make up the remainder of the top 50 most popular dogs in the UK. You'll need to do your own health research if you are attracted to one of these dogs, and you can find information and resources to help you in Part Three.

Popular breeds

21 Hungarian Vizsla
22 Chihuahua (Long Coat)
23 Boston Terrier
25 Dogue de Bordeaux
26 Bull Terrier
27 German Shorthaired Pointer
28 Rottweiler
29 Dobermann
30 Shar Pei
31 Yorkshire Terrier
32 Retriever (Flat Coated)
33 Tibetan Terrier
34 Maltese
35 Standard Poodle

36 Weimaraner
37 Bichon Frise
39 Great Dane
40 Dalmation
41 Toy Poodle
42 Shetland Sheepdog
43 Rhodesian Ridgeback
44 Newfoundland
45 Dachshund Miniature Long-Haired
46 Pomeranian
47 Siberian Husky
48 Cairn Terrier
49 Irish Setter
50 Rough Collie

Versatile Gundogs

There are three Short-Coated Gundogs that immediately stand out for me in this group of 30 dogs. And that is the Hungarian Vizsla, the German Shorthaired Pointer and the Weimaraner. All are from the Hunt, Point, Retriever (HPR) subgroup, also known as 'versatile' Gundogs. The Hungarian Vizsla in particular rivals the Labrador as an all-round companion for the outdoor-loving family. These are also breeds that will make good hunting companions for those with a sporting interest. Highly trainable, fairly quiet in nature and, while friendly, less pushy than some of our more popular gundog breeds, these are nice dogs. The Retriever (Flat Coated) is another good Gundog breed but currently suffers from high rates (over 50 per cent) of cancer, and the Irish Setter is a stunning dog but needs rather more exercise than the average family is able to provide. My current pick of these popular Gundog breeds is the Vizsla.

The Poodles

If you are looking for a little dog, the two smaller Poodle breeds are smart, affectionate and long-lived. They are also generally considered to be non-shedding

Poodles come in three sizes: Standard, Toy and Miniature.

so may be suitable for some people with allergies. While the Poodle coat can be challenging to manage if allowed to grow, a close clip every few weeks will keep it in order. Sometimes referred to as the French Poodle, we tend to associate the Poodle with France, but in fact his origins probably lie in Germany, where, according to some sources, the word *pudel* means to splash in water. Some people may be surprised to discover that the Poodle was originally a Gundog – specifically bred to retrieve – and working in water was one of his great talents.

The Poodle breed goes back a long way. Artwork by German artist Albrecht Dürer depicts the Poodle in drawings dating from the fifteenth century; it was well established as a popular pet in eighteenth-century Spain and France. Charles I was reputed to have owned a Poodle, and the breed was also a popular dog at the court of Louis XVI. In the longevity and mortality study of 2013, the Miniature Poodle is recorded as the longest-lived dog breed in the UK, with a lifespan of over 14 years. Some individuals live to 19 and beyond. However, many people are more familiar with the increasingly popular Poodle crossbreeds than they are with Poodles themselves.

Doodles and other Poodle crosses

There are a number of crossbreeds that are currently popular with puppy buyers. These are often referred to as 'designer dogs'. Unlike many mixed-breed dogs, which are of uncertain ancestry, designer dogs are first crosses between two purebred pedigree dogs from different breeds. The best-known and first to catch the wider public attention is the Labradoodle, a cross between the Labrador Retriever and a Standard Poodle. Other similar crosses, often involving smaller Poodle breeds, are now increasingly common. Many pedigree dog breeders frown on crossbreeding and see it as irresponsible. As discussed earlier in this book, designer dogs are especially contentious and they often fetch higher prices than puppies from their parent breeds.

The first Labradoodles were born in Australia in the 1950s. Wally Conron, a puppy breeding manager for the Royal Guide Dog Association of Australia, is credited with the creation of the Labradoodle in an attempt to create a 'hypoallergenic' dog that could be trained as a guide dog. He was successful in providing a family with a dog that did not trigger allergies, but in 2014 the *Independent* reported Conron as regretting what he did, claiming he felt that the popularity of Labradoodles is contributing to the problem of unwanted pets. In fact, I haven't found any evidence that this is the case, and much of the stigma attached to these crossbreeds seems undeserved.

The hypoallergenic coat

Although the first Labradoodles were born in an attempt to create a hypoallergenic coat, a Labradoodle may not necessarily inherit a Poodle coat. Labradors shed heavily, and some Labradoodles shed too. Always longer than a Labrador coat, the doodle coat varies from tight Poodle curls to a much looser, wavy coat or an even, fairly straight coat. The looser a Labradoodle's coat, the more it is likely to shed. And the tighter the coat, the more quickly it will become matted if not properly cared for. Because the Labradoodle coat is difficult to predict, getting a Labradoodle puppy is not a good idea if you are not fond of grooming or if you suffer from dog-hair allergies; the risk of getting a dog with a shedding coat is too great.

Other popular crossbreeds

Another popular crossbreed is the Cocker Spaniel/Poodle cross, or Cockapoo. As Cocker Spaniels and Poodles generally have a good temperament, and are relatively healthy breeds, the Cockapoo may be expected to be an even-tempered and healthy dog. As with the Labradoodle, the degree of shedding and coat type will vary between puppies even within the same litter. There are other first crosses that are becoming popular including the Cavachon (Cavalier King Charles x Bichon Frise), and the Puggle (Pug x Beagle).

In cases where one of the parent breeds has severely compromised conformation or genetic health, the first cross puppies *may* stand a better chance of a comfortable life than the sickly parent breed. The benefit to the breed on the other side of the mating may be less clear. A Puggle, for example, may be a healthier dog than his Pug parent, simply by virtue of possessing a muzzle, albeit a small one. He might not be such an improvement on his Beagle parent. My recommendation, if you are attracted to the idea of a crossbreed, is to make sure *both* parents are from a breed with minimal health issues. That way, your puppy should not be disadvantaged in any way.

Don't forget that part of a dog's temperament is dependent on his early upbringing, and much depends on the individual personalities of the father and mother. If the breeder did not take care to bring two good-natured dogs together, the puppies may have an uncertain temperament. The argument here is, of course, that a pedigree breeder may have more at stake than a Doodle breeder, and therefore be more likely to take care over such matters. Ultimately, you need to check out your breeder, just as you do any other breed, and if the breeder is inexperienced or has not been personally recommended to you, be very thorough and make sure you meet both parent dogs.

Lurchers

Traditionally thought of as the poacher's dog, the Lurcher originates from the concept of crossing a clever, trainable dog with a very fast dog. The idea is to combine speed and brains into one neat package. I am a big fan of sight hounds. I particularly love Lurchers, and have had the pleasure of sharing my life with two of these graceful, gentle dogs over the years. Many Lurchers are not first crosses but have been bred from a long line of Lurcher ancestors, and the original breeding may be lost in the mists of time. First crosses often involve a Collie crossed with a Greyhound or Whippet, but these are not the only options. Making a clever and very fast dog is obviously useful, but an additional benefit of outcrossing the sight hound is an improvement in coat. Whippets and Greyhounds have thin, short coats which offer little protection for a dog that may be running through undergrowth. Lurchers often have a thicker, more substantial coat. Like all sight hounds, Lurchers are well constructed and, if obtained from working lines and well exercised, are likely to be extremely fit and athletic dogs. Lurchers often look like a hairier version of a Greyhound or Whippet and many are very pretty dogs.

Jack Russell Terriers

Another breed I have had the pleasure of sharing my life with, only recently recognised by the Kennel Club and much beloved by rural folk across the UK, is the Jack Russell Terrier (JRT). With his brown-and-white patches, stumpy docked tail and cheeky nature, the Jack Russell is as much a part of the British countryside as wellington boots and Labradors. The news in 2015 that the Kennel Club would recognise this breed has been met with concern by many of this little Terrier's greatest fans, who fear that following form rather than fitness will be harmful to the breed.

Jack Russell Terriers are working dogs, bred and used for the purpose of bolting foxes from their underground homes. The JRT is often more of a wise worker than a fierce one, using cunning rather than force to eject the fox from his den – a feat he achieves by barking and threats, while keeping just out of reach of his quarry.

Because they are still, in the UK at least, widely used as working Terriers, the JRT has been bred for working ability, not for appearance. This means that he comes in quite a range of shapes and sizes: some with quite long legs, others shorter. Jack

Russell Terriers come in smooth- and rough-haired varieties. Some of the rough-haired dogs have longish coats that need thorough daily grooming to avoid matting. The longer hair also traps the dirt more easily. If your JRT has a typical Terrier enthusiasm for digging or exploring underground tunnels the occasional bath may be in order! Smooth-coated JRTs need very little in the way of coat care, a quick check for fleas and ticks and a brief whisk with a body brush is all that is required. It's a two-minute job. A typical working or farm-bred JRT usually has an easy-going, friendly nature, but the breed can also be found advertised by puppy farmers, or badly bred, so it makes sense to have your detective hat on when visiting a litter.

The dangers of wolf hybrids

On a more serious note, I need to mention a particular crossbreed that I caution against. That is a first cross between a wolf and a dog of any breed. Wolf hybrids are not dogs and, according to dog-bite experts, can be unpredictable and may exhibit a range of behaviours no longer found in our domesticated friends. Wolf hybrids are believed to be responsible for a disproportionate amount of attacks on human beings and, unlike most domestic dogs, may fail to give any warning that they feel threatened or need more space before launching an attack. Although they may be extremely beautiful, they are unsuitable pets.

Health issues in crossbreeds

Are crossbreeds healthier than purebred parents? Well, there is certainly less chance of them inheriting one of the recessive disorders lurking in either breed. However, finding a breeder that puts the same commitment and effort into the puppies may be more problematical. Any health issue shared by both parent breeds is a potential problem, and some health issues carried by only one of the parent breeds (for example, hip dysplasia) will be a problem too. So, for instance, if you are buying a Labradoodle puppy, your puppy's parents will both need to have been tested under the following two schemes:

- BVA/KC Hip Dysplasia Scheme
- BVA/KC/ISDS Eye Scheme.

These tests are crucial as both Labradors and Standard Poodles suffer from these conditions. It is also highly advisable that, as elbow dysplasia is increasingly common in Labradors, the Labrador parent also has this test:

- **BVA/KC Elbow Dysplasia Scheme.**

The use of the Kennel Club's health testing schemes by the breeder of designer dogs is a great sign that they are taking their responsibilities just as seriously as any purebred breeder would. You can find out the tests your crossbred puppy's parents should have certificates for by looking up both parent breeds on the Kennel Club's website.

With any mixed-breed mating there will be a significant reduction in the risk of nasty hidden recessive genes meeting a matching partner and making your dog unwell with a known or new genetic condition. Temperament is determined as we have seen partly by inheritance and partly by upbringing. If you can find a dedicated, caring breeder who makes the effort to thoroughly socialise their puppies, and if both parents have good temperaments, you have as much chance of getting a good-natured puppy as you do with a purebred puppy from a breed known to have a good temperament.

Finding your puppy

There is no doubt that there are some bad breeders who have jumped on the designer dog bandwagon, in just the same way that some bad breeders have jumped on the bandwagon for fashionable breeds like the French Bulldog. This is inevitable when the demand for puppies pushes prices up. It is simply not true to say that all designer dog breeders are puppy farmers, or bad breeders. Nor is the breeding of purebred pedigree puppies any guarantee that your chosen breeder is breeding responsibly, or that the breed of puppy they are selling is a fundamentally healthy one.

Which brings us to the all-important question of where to find your puppy. So far, we have talked about the type of dog that might be best suited to your family, and looked at a variety of different dog breeds to help you make up your mind. In Part Three, we'll move on to the final stage of your search and help you to track down the puppy of your dreams. We'll look at all the different places where puppies can be bought and sold and figure out how to go about completing this final stage of your journey.

Finding Your Perfect Puppy

1

Where Do Puppies Come From?

For many of us, the first thing we do when we want to find something is search the internet. And this, more often than not, is the first step people take in trying to find a litter of puppies. There are a number of reasons that this is not a good idea, at least, not to begin with. You can certainly make use of the internet, but first you need to know what you are doing.

There are a number of different sources of puppies for sale throughout the UK and beyond, and the first thing to remember is that there is very little regulation at all about who can sell puppies and the standards that people who are breeding from dogs should meet. Most of the regulation in Britain relates to basic animal welfare legislation. In other words, a breeder must meet their dogs' basic needs and make sure they don't suffer. There are no legal requirements for good breeding practices, such as arranging matings with low coefficients of inbreeding or on running health checks on the parents. Those breeding more than a few litters a year have to register with their local authority and have their premises inspected, but this doesn't apply to many dog breeders.

This means that puppy buyers must not only educate themselves on what defines a healthy puppy, but they must also know how to recognise an establishment where a puppy may not have received optimum care. In other words, you need to become a bit of a detective. We've looked at what defines a great puppy in Part One. In this chapter we are going to look at the various ways in which puppies can be purchased and their pros and cons, so you can distinguish between a great provider of puppies and the kind of puppy breeders that you should avoid.

Essentially there are five sources of puppies in the UK:

1. **Dog rescue centres**
2. **Commercial breeders**
3. **Hobby or enthusiast breeders**
4. **Pet stores**
5. **Home breeders.**

Each of these different types of puppy provider may encourage sales of their puppies in different ways, including online advertisements, building up a reputation, advertising in newspapers and so on. And you need to be able to tell the difference between them. Let's look at each one in turn.

Dog rescue centres

If you are lucky, you may find a litter of puppies at a shelter or dog rescue. If you are even luckier, you may find a puppy of the breed you are specifically hoping for at a dog rescue. But it's fair to say that puppies tend to be snapped up pretty quickly and getting a rescue puppy can be a bit of a hit-and-miss affair.

There are downsides to getting a rescue puppy. If the puppy is an abandoned mixed-breed, you won't usually have much idea what he is going to look like when he is an adult. You won't know how big he'll get or how much he'll weigh. If he is a mixed breed, his coefficient of inbreeding is likely to be zero, and that bodes well for his genetic health, but he may not have had a great start in life when it comes to nutrition and socialisation. If he is purebred, and purebred puppies do end up in rescues sometimes, you probably won't have any health clearances for him, and buying a purebred puppy without health clearances is, in some breeds, a risky move.

Rescuing a dog can be very satisfying. It is great to know that you have given an abandoned dog the chance of a good life. Whether or not you choose to go down that route may depend on how concerned you are about the final appearance of your dog, how much the idea of rescuing appeals to you, and how willing you are to take a bit of a chance. Puppies don't come up for adoption with anything like the frequency of older dogs, and tend to be adopted quite quickly, but if you put your name down with an animal shelter or rescue centre you may be lucky.

Most animal rescue centres require some kind of financial contribution, but this is likely to be quite a bit less than the cost of a pedigree puppy. Most dog rescues have quite strict conditions for prospective adopters. You can expect a home visit from the organisation concerned and some intensive questioning. These questions are designed to eliminate potential adopters who are not ready to bring a dog into their lives, but they may also exclude certain categories of potential puppy parent. Many rescue centres, for example, won't allow adoptions by families where everyone works full-time, even if the family is willing and able to provide daycare in a crèche or with a local dog walker. If the first rescue society you approach won't take you on, it is worth trying others. There are many different rescue centres throughout the UK, some breed specific, some run by charities, some privately owned and managed, and they all have different rules. They have different standards too, so you will need to make sure you ask plenty of questions about any potential puppies and find out what kind of support is offered to you and your family after you bring your puppy home. You can find lists of rescue organisations in the breed sections on the Kennel Club website and many breed specific websites, such as my www.thelabradorsite.com for example, also carry lists of rescue organisations for that breed, together with their contact details.

Commercial breeders

Otherwise known as puppy farmers, these are the commercial breeders who are breeding *purely* for profit. There are enthusiast breeders who are sufficiently successful to profit from their endeavours too, but I will consider those separately. One of the downsides of buying a puppy from a puppy farm is that the puppy may have had little in the way of loving care. Many puppy farms do not carry out health screening on their breeding stock, because health tests are expensive and they eat into profits. Many puppy farms do not socialise their puppies properly, or provide much in the way of good medical care, so that you risk getting a dog that may be sickly, or grows up to be fearful and potentially dangerous. On a more general note, puppy farms are unhappy places for the female dogs used in their breeding programme because they serve no purpose than producing puppies. Most of these female dogs get little in the way of companionship or exercise. Finally, puppy farmers do not offer after-sales support or a lifetime return policy to their puppy buyers.

The driving force behind a puppy farm is profit. The main reason not to buy from a puppy farm is that the welfare of the female dogs producing puppies is compromised. Their lives lack companionship, purpose and exercise. Access to healthcare may be minimal, and once their breeding days are over they will be discarded. The care of puppies may also be substandard, socialisation and health screening may be absent or minimal and this has adverse effects on the temperament and health of the dogs concerned.

For all these reasons, puppy buyers need to avoid puppy farmers when searching for the dog of their dreams. We'll have a look in more detail at how to recognise a puppy farm in the next chapter, because it is not as easy as you might think, and because it is important to be aware that many puppy farmers sell their puppies via a third party.

Hobby or enthusiast breeders

A dog breeding enthusiast usually has a particular interest in either exhibiting their dogs, or in working those dogs in some kind of sport or activity, agility for example, or Gundog fieldwork – often in a competitive context. The breed enthusiast may breed one or two litters a year in order to raise a puppy that will help them achieve their aims on the bench or in the field. The rest of the litter will usually be sold as companions to the general public. It is these puppies that most people are thinking of when they talk of buying a puppy from a responsible breeder.

It is hard to make money out of breeding from female dogs without cutting corners, so most of these hobby breeders either have a 'day job' or they have reached such a high level in competition that they can make a living from the stud fees acquired through mating their male dogs. A few hobby breeders do make a living from breeding dogs, and they tend to straddle a precarious line between hobby breeder or enthusiast and commercial breeder. To distinguish between them, first and foremost you need to look at the way the female dogs in their care live their lives. We'll look at that in more detail in the next chapter.

Many hobby breeders are not up to date with the latest research and are still focused on line breeding (inbreeding), so you will need to look carefully at the coefficient of inbreeding of any litter you are interested in. Hobby breeders who are keen exhibitors of their breed may not be the best place to buy puppies from a structurally compromised breed, due to exaggerations in conformation in some breeds. What you will often get from many hobby or enthusiast breeders is a high quality of puppy care and excellent after-sales service, which is an important benefit for the new puppy owner.

Pet stores

Although many of the smaller pet shops no longer sell dogs, pet stores or shops that sell puppies can still be found in most large towns and cities. These puppies are kept on the store's premises and may be put out on display for the public to look at. There are many problems with pet store puppies, not least of which is that they are almost all sourced from puppy farms. No reputable hobby breeder would ever sell one of their precious puppies to a pet shop, so all the problems that apply to farmed puppies apply to pet shop puppies too. With the additional disadvantage that you won't be able to see the mother or have any idea at all how your puppy has been cared for or socialised. Puppies in pet shops are also sometimes imported from abroad, and it can be very hard to know whether these puppies have been imported legally. It is simply a very bad idea indeed to purchase any puppy from such an establishment.

A study published in February 2016 showed that puppies purchased from pet stores were more likely to be aggressive, supporting the assumption that such puppies may be badly bred or that socialisation is absent or inadequate in these dogs. Don't be tempted to try and 'save' the puppy. Remember that buying a puppy from a pet shop tells the pet shop owner that it is worth replacing that puppy with another. This in turn encourages puppy farmers to breed yet more puppies. The same applies to buying puppies from street markets and car boot sales. No matter how sweet or appealing such a puppy may be, don't give in to temptation. You will simply be perpetuating an unpleasant trade in substandard and neglected animals.

Home breeders

Often looked down upon by hobby breeders, a home breeder is someone who has had a litter of puppies, either planned or by accident, from a family pet, and who is probably not intending to repeat the experience. There are both pros and cons of buying from a home breeder. If the puppies were not planned, the parents won't have been screened for common diseases in their breeds. Even if the puppies were planned, many inexperienced breeders fail to carry out these important tests, either through ignorance or to avoid the costs involved. The breeder's inexperience may also mean that the puppies have not had the best care. They might not have been wormed at the right intervals or given an ideal diet; they might not have had the best start to socialisation too.

On the other hand, there can be considerable advantages to a home-bred puppy from someone's pet, especially where the family have taken the time and trouble to learn how to do the very best for their bitch and her puppies. I didn't know very much about what to expect when I bred my first litter, but I bought myself a good book, listened to the advice of experienced breeders and learnt fast. At some point, most hobby breeders started out this way. In a loving family environment, puppies are likely to be well handled, and to have been exposed to plenty of visitors, household noises and disturbances, and be generally well cared for. So provided they have carried out the necessary health tests, don't discount an inexperienced breeder out of hand.

Routes to success

I hope I have convinced you not to purchase your puppy from a puppy farm or from a pet shop. So what we are left with are three sources of puppies:

1. **Dog rescues**
2. **Hobby or enthusiast breeders**
3. **Home breeders.**

The prospect of picking a puppy is an exciting one, and the final stage in our journey. But, before that, we need to find a litter of puppies to choose from. In a well-bred litter, all the puppies will normally be healthy and strong, but making the final decisions on your choice of dog, and finding a litter to match them, is not always straightforward. That's what the next chapter is all about.

2

How to Find a Litter

n this chapter we're going to look at the best way to find a great litter of puppies – a litter with the potential to provide you with the right dog for your family. Ideally we are looking for a litter bred from well-structured, genetically healthy, good-natured parents. A litter that has been well nourished, well socialised and that has a great chance of a long and healthy life. This could be a litter produced by an experienced breed enthusiast, or it could be a litter raised by a knowledgeable and caring pet owner. If the breed is one that has been exaggerated in one or more respects by those breeding for the show ring, then a pet owner may be a better bet. But in many cases, a breed enthusiast will be ideal. Breeders that have an established reputation may never need to advertise their puppies, but many newer breeders do, and we'll be looking at the best places to find advertisements for quality puppies in this chapter. We'll also look at how to find those breeders that don't advertise and jump the queue to a quality puppy.

Responsible breeders will never sell their dog's puppies through pet shops.

🐾 Your ideal dog

Before we begin thinking about what defines a good breeder or a great litter, and how to go about finding one, we need to have a shortlist with one or two of the breeds or crossbreeds you are interested in. Your choice of breed will influence where we begin our search, so let's get that shortlist sorted out now. Let's start by writing down what you would like your dog to look like when he is fully grown. It's a good idea to describe your future friend in some detail. Does he have upright ears? A short coat or long? Curly or straight? How tall is he? And how much does he weigh? Do you love slender, elegant dogs, or favour a more chunky appearance? Are you a big dog fan, or would you prefer a smaller, more portable friend?

Next, try to envisage the kind of activities you and your dog might enjoy together. Do you want to take him shooting, or run marathons with him? Do you fancy having a go at flyball or obedience training? Do you plan to take long hiking holidays in the mountains? Will your dog like playing Frisbee with your children? Riding in the car? Digging on the beach? Is your dog going to spend large periods of time on his own or can he be a dog that really loves company? Are any members of your family unsteady on their feet (toddlers or the elderly), or will a boisterous dog not be a problem?

Picture your dog at home. Does his bed occupy a large part of your kitchen, can you see him sprawled out on the sofa? Does he shed, and does that worry you? Is there someone in the family with allergies? Do you have a passion for grooming or are you looking for a dog with a short, easy-care coat?

🐾 Check the reviews

There is a lot to think about. Write it all down. You may well end up with a completely different dog than the one you imagine, but there are a lot of dogs out there and it's time to make up your mind! Once you have an idea of the kind of characteristics your dog might have, it's time to take another look at the review section and at the top 20 most popular dog breeds in the UK. Note down features of dogs that will eliminate them from your list. Dogs that are unsuitable companions for your children, or that can't cope with much exercise, for example.

The chances are that your future friend is in that top 20. And if he isn't, you'll have a clearer picture of what you do and don't like when you have looked through these 20 breeds. There are representatives of every group there, and once you have made your choice, it's time to start tracking down potential litters. Before we do that, let's just make sure you don't slip into the trap that many others fall into each year, and end up at a puppy farm.

How to avoid a puppy farm

Perhaps surprisingly, most of us would find it difficult to recognise a puppy farm if we found one. There is a general perception of puppy farms as being squalid places where dogs are confined in horrific conditions, and where designer puppies are churned out and sold for exorbitant prices. These kinds of sad places do exist. However, for the most part this is far from the truth. Many puppy farms are breeding pedigree dogs that are kept in relatively clean and tidy conditions. They are inspected and approved by the local authority and their puppies are registered with the Kennel Club. And many puppy-farmed puppies are sold through 'middle men' who buy, and sell on, the puppies privately.

A puppy farm is defined by the primary purpose of its breeding stock. Usually these are all female dogs, and their primary purpose is the production of puppies. You cannot clearly define a puppy farm by the number of animals kept at the establishment (though this may be an indication) or by the conditions in which the animals are kept. This is an important distinction to make. A breeder who is not farming puppies keeps bitches whose primary purpose is either as a companion for the family, or participation in some kind of sport or activity. This might include obedience competitions, working trials, field trials (Gundogs) or exhibiting at dog shows. Such a breeder may house some of her bitches in kennels, and she may at times have more than one litter. This does not make her a puppy farmer if her female dogs have a fulfilling and happy life.

Some breeders do not provide good care for their puppies, through ignorance or circumstance, and obviously you'll want to avoid these breeders, but lack of quality care alone does not mean they are puppy farmers. On the other side of the coin, there are puppy farmers that masquerade as responsible breeders. Their kennels may be gleaming and their puppies immaculate. Some of their dogs may be exhibited at dog shows, and they may even own a champion or two. But if they are breeding for financial profit *and* depriving their bitches of a full and happy life in the company of human beings, they are puppy farming.

If this sounds confusing it's because it is! Recognising a puppy farm can be difficult, especially if you are denied access to the animal's living quarters and if the puppy farmer brings the puppies into the house for viewing purposes. Pet shops and puppy merchants are now becoming wise to increasing public awareness of how puppy farms work, and puppy sellers may arrange for viewings to take place well away from the breeding centre. A recent televised undercover report on puppy farmers confirmed that some puppy farmers, or 'middle men' who buy puppies from them, will bring puppies into a family home in a residential area for viewing purposes so that it appears they are being cared for in a normal environment. The reporters filmed puppy sellers 'borrowing' the mother of the puppies for a few days while puppies are sold to unsuspecting visitors, and returning the bitch to the puppy farm afterwards. This is perhaps the most important argument for visiting a true breed enthusiast when you purchase a puppy, rather than someone who claims to have simply bred from their pet, unless of course you know them personally. There are, however, a few clues that will help you decide whether or not the puppy you are looking at is from a puppy farm.

The key when making an assessment is to focus on the mother dog and her relationship with the person selling the puppies:

- **Does the female dog know her name, is she obedient, does she have a relationship with the owner?**
- **Is the owner affectionate towards her, does she enjoy talking about her?**
- **Persistently steer the conversation back to the mother dog. What kind of dog was she when growing up, what kind of activities do they do together?**
- **Look around you. Does the mother dog have toys? Is there evidence of her around the home, hair on the furniture, a collar and lead hanging behind the kitchen door, photos of her on the mantelpiece? People always photograph their dogs. Be suspicious if these things are absent.**

Most people are so wrapped up in talking about and looking at the puppies that they don't think to look at the mother–breeder relationship. There is no need for you to fall into this trap. If in doubt walk away. There is always another litter and another day. A reputable breeder will not try to pressure you into making a decision on your first visit. On the contrary, many good breeders won't allow you to take a puppy on a first visit, even if the puppy is ready to leave, but will ask you to sleep on your decision. Most responsible breeders will not even ask for a deposit. It goes without saying that you should never, ever agree to meet a puppy seller halfway with a puppy, so that you don't get to visit the premises or the mother of the puppies, no matter how convenient and appealing that may be.

Puppy advertisements

A quick internet search for puppies of any breed or crossbreed will bring up a number of websites dedicated to puppy sales advertisements for puppies of all breeds. Many are general 'pet sales' websites, and kittens and other pet animals can also be found there. Some of these websites will also provide basic advice for puppy buyers, such as making sure you always see a puppy with his mother. Treading a path through internet and newspaper advertisements is tricky for a newcomer to dogs, because there is little indication of the kind of establishment that the puppy is being raised in, the credentials of the breeder or the provenance of the puppies. Many people will tell you that no decent breeder would advertise their puppies on such a website, and there is some truth in this. It is also true that many of the advertisements on such websites may be placed there by puppy farmers. Commercial breeders may also post on more general district sites. At the time of writing, you can find puppy adverts on Gumtree, for example.

A less experienced or knowledgeable breeder might be tempted to post an advert for a perfectly nice litter on such a site, but it will be difficult to discriminate between them, and there are easier ways to find a good puppy. For this reason, I suggest you view such adverts with caution. If you do decide to visit a litter of puppies advertised in this way, copy out the checklist at the end of this chapter and get as many answers as possible to your questions before travelling to visit the puppies.

So, if puppy farms are out, and adverts are a bad idea, where are you supposed to find a breeder with a nice litter of puppies?

The responsible breeder

The standard advice given out to puppy buyers is often 'find a "responsible" breeder'. In many cases your ideal starting point will be a breed enthusiast, but not in every case. This is because the definition of 'responsible breeder' is changing. Not so long ago, a responsible breeder was someone who health-tested their breeding stock, competed in the show ring or in sporting activities with their dog, took good care of their puppies and offered long-term aftercare for their puppy buyers. Most breed enthusiasts are heavily into health testing. If the main problem with the breed you are interested in is inherited diseases *not associated with structure*, then for your puppy's safety a breed enthusiast is still likely to be your best bet.

Most breed enthusiasts are also keen exhibitors and like to enter their dogs in conformation shows. These breeders measure their success in breeding by their wins in the show ring and they measure their *dogs* against the breed standard. This is a big problem for breeds with serious structural defects, especially where those defects or disabilities are becoming more exaggerated as the years go by. This is because the very people who should be responsible for improving the breed are the ones who are letting the breed down. So, if you are attracted to a breed whose major health issues are structural ones, flat-faced or short-legged breeds, for example, you might stand a better chance of finding a healthier puppy by looking for a home-bred dog, or even a crossbred dog of the same type. This is where you have to use the knowledge you have now gained to make an informed decision.

If you are also concerned about the future of the breed, and of the chances of your puppy being affected by lack of genetic diversity passed down from his parents, you also need to find a breeder who is abreast of the latest understanding of pedigree dog health issues. Nowadays a truly responsible breeder needs to go much further than just health testing the parents of her puppies. A responsible breeder:

- **Avoids using popular sires on their bitches**
- **Understands the coefficient of inbreeding and no longer 'line breeds' their dogs**
- **Knows that he cannot health test his breed out of trouble**
- **Does not breed from dogs that have serious structural problems**
- **Puts the genetic and structural health of his breeding stock as a priority**

This breeder is harder to find, but worth looking for. One way to discover how responsible and up to date a breeder is, is simply to talk to them, and ask for their views on the Kennel Club's Mate Select programme or the Institute of Biology's website. A good breeder will be making use of both these facilities to ensure their dogs are not too inbred and that they are up to date with the latest developments in their breed. If they have not heard of these resources, or don't think them worthwhile, that is not a good sign. You can also look in the places where these breeders gather. There are Facebook groups, for example, run by the Institute of Canine Biology, for breeders interested in improving their knowledge and understanding of genetics, and other groups for breeders who support outcrossing. It is well worth joining and contributing to these. Many good breeders will also make use of the RSPCA/BVA AWF Puppy Contract and Puppy Information Pack, which is a record of the thought they have given to their puppies' care, and/or have their own puppy information documents which you can ask to see in advance of collecting your puppy. The Kennel Club also has a special scheme that sets standards for pedigree dog breeders called the Assured Breeder Scheme.

The Kennel Club Assured Breeder Scheme

The KC's Assured Breeder Scheme acknowledges breeders who reach certain standards of care and who actively participate in the Kennel Club's recommended health-testing schemes for their breed. These are breeders who provide the kind of service that many people believe is already implied by the wider pool of those breeding KC registered puppies. Many of us think that some of the standards embraced in the Assured Breeder Scheme, such as an insistence on certain minimum health tests for breeding animals, should be a requirement for KC registration of puppies, but currently this is not the case. While membership of the Assured Breeder Scheme means that certain minimum standards are implied, *not* belonging to the Assured Breeder Scheme doesn't mean a breeder has low standards, just that he or she has not joined the scheme. Some breeders with very high standards simply do not believe the scheme is right for them.

Let's assume that you are looking for a dog that has a basically healthy construction, and therefore a breed enthusiast, probably an exhibitor of his breed, is the person you are looking for. Where do you go to find that person?

Breed clubs

When the pursuit of the ideal purebred pedigree dog began in earnest, many breed clubs were formed. As each new breed of dog was recognised and registered, a club consisting of breed enthusiasts formed to set standards, hold dog shows and oversee field events. Many of those clubs are now over a hundred years old and still exist today. Many more have sprung up more recently. There are often regional clubs for different parts of the country and popular breeds may have as many as ten or more breed clubs in the UK.

You need to be a member of such a club to enter competitions and, to progress with campaigning or competing your dogs, you need to enter many competitions. Each club holds a limited number annually, so if you want to compete, membership of multiple clubs is essential.

Some breed clubs are very active in trying to improve their breed's health problems. The Dachshund Club, for example, have a comprehensive website addressing the very serious problems in the breed. Some breed clubs, however, seem to be in complete denial of the fact that their dogs are disabled or disadvantaged by their breed standard. And while the Kennel Club does try to influence breeders, it seems that there is currently no governing body with the will, and means, to force radical changes in structure on clubs overseeing the breeding of dogs with disabilities.

Because breed clubs vary in their approach to health and welfare, you'll need to take each one on its own merits. But they can be a very good way of finding a dedicated and caring breeder from whom to buy your puppy, especially in breeds where the structure of the dog is basically sound.

A great way to begin looking for a puppy is to look at dogs that have recently been mated, or at matings planned in the weeks ahead. A dog is pregnant for nine weeks, and puppies can go to their new homes at eight weeks old. So if you find a female dog that has just been mated, you will have a wait of some 17 weeks. It is worth finding more than one such mating, because sometimes things go wrong, the female dog may turn out not to be pregnant after all at her five-week scan, for example, and then you will be back to square one.

Steps to take

Your search for a puppy needs to start with a planned mating or pregnancy. The truth is, great litters get booked up early and popular breeders have long waiting lists. Unless yours is a *very* numerically popular breed indeed *and* you are searching in early to mid-summer, you are not going to find a quality puppy by looking for a 'puppy'. The good ones are all spoken for before or soon after birth.

Here are the steps you need to take:

1 Approaching a breed club

Lists of breed clubs are held on the Kennel Club website, and most breed clubs have a website of their own. Look for a list of committee members and note down their contact details. If you are looking for a working-strain dog, contact the committee members concerned in that side of the breed. Email each new contact you find, and tell them you are looking for a puppy, and what you want the puppy for (show, work, pet). Don't give them your life history at this point (that comes later), but just ask to be put in touch with club members who might have a litter or be planning a litter in the next few weeks. Ask each breeder to also let you know of any matings they have planned for their stud dogs. Then you wait – this is the hard part. The more people you contact, the sooner you'll start getting responses and be able to begin building your list.

2 Making a list

Your list of potential litters needs to contain several dates. The date the female dog is due in season (if she hasn't been mated already), the date of mating and the due date for the puppies. Mating takes place a couple of weeks into the bitch's season and puppies are born approximately nine weeks later.

With a popular breed you'll build up a list of at least a dozen potential matings quite quickly. With a rarer breed this stage can take months. You'll also want to make a note of the answers to important health questions.

3 Check the coefficient of inbreeding

Check the COI of each planned mating, and make a note of it on your list. It should be under 5 per cent as this is the level at which the deleterious effects of inbreeding become evident. You can use the Kennel Club's Mate Select tool for this purpose. Select your breed from the list provided then simply enter the kennel names of the parents of the litter into the inbreeding coefficient calculator.

4 Check health test results

Make a note of the health test results of both parent dogs.

5 Note down any other influencing factors that matter to you

Expected colours, for example.

6 If you are happy, confirm your interest

Expect to be grilled in some detail by the breeder at some point as to your suitability to own one of his precious babies. If that doesn't happen, be very suspicious.

7 Visiting the parents of your puppy

It is essential that you meet the mother of your puppies. Whether this is before or after the puppies are born is between you and the breeder, but meet her you must. And I would give the highest priority to litters where you can also meet the father. This is because temperament is partly inherited and because two delightfully good-natured parents gives you a much higher chance of an equally good-natured puppy. Meeting both parents is doubly important in breeds where outstanding temperament and absence of guarding behaviour is not a feature of the breed.

8 Check credentials

Ask to see proof of the relevant health tests and results. Decide for yourself what is relevant by researching problems in that breed. You can find health information in the Breed Reviews section of this book, and resources for researching other breeds at the end of Part Three. If you are buying a puppy from two pedigree dogs of the same breed, the litter should be registered with the Kennel Club. Failure to register could mean that the breeder has failed to meet the basic requirements of the KC for registration purposes. The parent might be too closely related, for example, or the bitch may have had too many litters or be too old.

The breeder should email or post you copies of certificates. Make sure you see these *before you visit* the puppies. This is so important because once you have held a puppy in your arms, a large proportion of your rational brain will cease to function, and you will not make decisions founded in common sense and logic.

9 Four weeks before the birth

If your search has begun early enough you will need to confirm your interest in writing once the pregnancy has been confirmed, often by ultrasound at around five weeks after mating. Some breeders may ask for a deposit at this point; many will not want one until the puppies are a couple of weeks old. Some will never accept deposits at all, and this shows confidence (and a long waiting list).

Now all that remains is to wait for the birth of your puppy. You'll be able to visit the puppies once they are four or five weeks old and you may be given the opportunity to choose which puppy you take home. That's what the next chapter is all about. In the meantime let's just summarise what we have covered so far and give you some tips.

Key points

1. Shortlist breeds that are known for their good temperament
2. Avoid breeds with major structural problems
3. Never buy a puppy from a vehicle, shop or market
4. Never buy a puppy without meeting its mother
5. Unless your breed has a physical disability built into the breed standard, begin your search with a breed club
6. Start your search early, with a planned mating
7. Prioritise breeders who use the RSPCA/BVA AWF Puppy Contract and Information Pack
8. Check the coefficient of inbreeding for each litter
9. Don't visit puppies until you have ticked off the health tests and seen copies of certificates
10. If you find a litter in an advertisement, focus on the mother dog, not the puppies.

3
Picking Your Puppy

Choosing between two perfect puppies is a difficult decision.

You have found a litter of beautiful puppies, with great conformation, from parents that are not too closely related, being raised in a caring and knowledgeable environment. Now comes the exciting part. Once you have chosen a great litter of puppies you may be given the opportunity to pick out the puppy of your dreams from seven or eight squirming bundles of cuteness. I say *may* be given, because if you have booked a puppy from a popular breeder, the choice of puppy may be taken out of your hands. We'll look at that in a moment. But first let's assume you are given a choice. How are you supposed to decide?

It may seem like an impossible task and you may feel under a lot of pressure to make the right choice. After all it is a really important decision and, if you have followed the steps in this book, the chances are good that this little dog will be a part of your life for the next decade or more. Fortunately, this is one of the many occasions where a good choice of breeder should stand you in good stead.

I want to reassure you, first and foremost, that you don't need to be an expert to choose the right puppy. Your biggest task, finding a great breeder and the right litter, is already behind you. The chances are high that *all* the puppies in your chosen litter will grow up to be fantastic, healthy companions. In other words, the work you have done so far should take some of the pressure out of this decision, and you can relax in the knowledge that your choice now isn't going to make or break the future.

Nevertheless, there are some things you'll find it helpful to consider when choosing a puppy, so let's get straight to them. We'll be looking at the difference between owning a male dog and owning a female dog, at trying to distinguish between the temperament of different puppies, and at checking puppies for health problems. But the first dilemma that sometimes greets and surprises a new puppy buyer is being offered more than one puppy.

One puppy or two?

Sometimes a family deliberately set out to buy two puppies at the same time. And sometimes a breeder will offer a second puppy to a family when they are choosing their puppy. There are two issues to consider here. One is the pros and cons of raising two puppies at once, the other is the concerns it raises about the breeder who offers this option. Let's take the pros and cons of raising two puppies at once.

If you intend to have more than one dog in your life, then there are practical advantages and disadvantages to getting both dogs at the same time and from the same litter. There are also some less practical, but equally important, disadvantages that you might not have thought of. On the practical side, two puppies keep each other company when you can't be there. They are less likely to cry at night during the first few days in their new home, and may be less inclined to cry when you go out and leave them alone during the day. They will also play together and amuse each other, which may seem like a great idea. Unfortunately, the downsides can outweigh these advantages, especially after the first week when most singleton puppies will have settled into their new homes.

Two puppies complicates things, and those complications can go on and on.

House training two puppies at once can be tricky. There are double the accidents to clear up, and because puppies like to wee and poop where other dogs have done so, if one puppy has an accident the other puppy will be encouraged to do the same. This inconvenience is temporary and fairly minor.

Socialisation involves taking your puppy into many different situations in the first few weeks after he joins your family. You'll be going to the bus station, riding on a train, visiting town centres, schools, country shows, schools and shops, and lots of different friends. Unless you have a team of helpers, this is more difficult to manage with two dogs than one. Your puppies also need to be able to cope with these situations without their little sibling, so some of this process needs to be done once with one puppy alone and again with the other. Again, this is a fairly short-lived issue.

The biggest practical problem is obedience training two puppies. You cannot effectively train a dog to any kind of high standard with another dog present. At least not to begin with. When your dogs are learning to walk on a loose leash, for example, you have to take each dog out on his own, ideally twice daily, and then repeat the whole session with the other dog. Only when each dog has reached a reasonable standard of obedience on his own can you introduce the distraction of another dog. The point at which I am most often contacted by owners of two litter brothers or sisters is when they run into difficulties trying to train two dogs at once. Training separately to begin with is an essential that most people did not bargain for; it is time consuming and often frustrating.

The most important problem that can arise when two puppies of the same age are adopted together is a phenomenon known as littermate syndrome. It is a difficult problem to deal with and common enough that any experienced breeder will have heard about it. Littermate syndrome occurs when two puppies become closely bonded, sometimes to the detriment of their relationship with their human family. Often one puppy becomes the leader, and the other the follower. It can affect the confidence of the more subservient puppy, who becomes very dependent on his brother or sister and finds it hard to cope when his littermate is absent.

Being offered two puppies from the same litter also raises questions about the breeder's own motives and experience. Forming a good relationship with a puppy is an important part of raising a healthy, happy, biddable and well-behaved dog. Many experts believe that this is much harder to do when two pups from the same litter are raised together. For this reason, most experienced and responsible breeders would never sell two puppies to the same family. Even if the breeder is simply ignorant about

In a well-bred litter, all the puppies will be equally worthy.

littermate syndrome, it is a cause for concern to be offered two puppies at once.

There is no doubt that it is possible to make a success of raising littermates, but it takes effort and commitment. You'll need to dedicate a lot of time to interacting with your puppies separately, training them separately, and to teaching each to cope without the other. If this is to be your first puppy, my recommendation would be to stick to one puppy at this point, and perhaps consider getting another when your first dog is two or three years old.

Male or female?

As small puppies, apart from a slight difference in average weight, there is little to choose between a male and a female pup. But, of course, puppies grow into adult dogs, and there are some differences in temperament between unaltered adult dogs of different genders. These differences are less important than you might think, especially in our modern world, where most dogs are secured within their owner's property when at home and supervised outdoors throughout their lives. One way to minimise the differences that do exist is to neuter your pet at an early age, but recent evidence shows us that this approach is not without its problems. We'll look at this in a moment, and the outcome is that some dog owners are choosing to leave their puppies entire (delaying or avoiding neutering), at least for the first couple of years. For this reason we need to take gender differences in entire adult dogs into account.

Differences in appearance between male and female dogs

Male dogs are usually a little heavier and taller than female dogs and, if not neutered at a young age, often have a much more masculine appearance, with chunkier, broader faces. Some people prefer this to the daintier, more feminine look of an adult female dog. This gender difference is more striking in some breeds than in others. Neutering at an early age has a feminising effect on the appearance of male dogs and make this difference less noticeable.

Differences in behaviour between male and female dogs

Adult male dogs that have not been neutered are strongly attracted to the scent of a female dog in season. A male dog can smell such a female at considerable distances and will try hard to reach her. This means that if your garden or yard is not secure, your male dog will undoubtedly roam. Some adult female dogs will roam too, especially when they are in season, though this is less common. Furthermore, some neutered dogs will also roam if not confined. Therefore, the only way to avoid roaming entirely is to fence your dog in.

Some people think that male dogs are more likely to exhibit unwanted sexual behaviour such as humping, or to fight or bite than female dogs, and that they are harder to train. A US study into dog bite injuries showed that male dogs were more likely to bite than females. But there were complicating factors. For example, a quarter of the bites were by unrestrained dogs roaming away from the owner's property, and we know that female dogs are far less likely to roam. This could account for the difference. Other studies have shown that gender differences in aggression only apply to certain breeds. The truth is that most well-raised and well-socialised males are not interested in picking fights with or humping other dogs, and are just as easy to train as their sisters. Humping is not a simple sexual behaviour and puppies (and adults) of both sexes may do this in play and out of habit.

Adult females in season

Adult female dogs that have not been neutered usually come into season twice a year, and each season or heat lasts three to four weeks. During that time a female dog has a blood-stained vaginal discharge that you probably won't want on your furniture or carpets. If you can easily keep your dog on washable floors it won't be much of an issue, and some females keep themselves so clean that you'll hardly notice the discharge at all. Other dogs are less fastidious and will drip all over your floors.

The effect of neutering on health and behaviour

Neutering in male dogs involves a minor operation. It reduces roaming, and may reduce the incidence of embarrassing sexual behaviour such as humping if carried out early enough in a dog's life. But unfortunately there are also disadvantages. In male dogs, some studies have shown that neutering increases the risk of behavioural problems and aggression. This is probably because it deprives the dog of testosterone, which is a confidence building hormone.

In female dogs, neutering is a more involved and more expensive operation. Most importantly, in both sexes neutering has been shown in some breeds to increase the risk of serious joint problems such as cranial cruciate ligament disease and hip dysplasia. Neutering has also been shown to increase the risk of several types of cancer, such as lymphosarcoma and hemangiosarcoma, in some breeds. The increase in cancer risk may be more significant in female dogs.

The effects of neutering vary from one breed to another, and between males and females, and this research is still ongoing, but in male dogs it is looking as though neutering may have a net disadvantage to the dog in terms of general health and behaviour. In female dogs the risks of neutering have to be weighed against the fact that neutering in females also conveys important protection against pyometra. This is a serious and potentially fatal infection of the uterus, which affects up to 20 per cent of entire females. Neutered female dogs cannot develop pyometra, nor do they continue to come into season, which means that you do not have to worry about keeping your neutered female dog isolated for three or four weeks every six months.

Deciding whether to neuter in advance

It is important to think about neutering before picking a puppy because this may influence your decision about male versus female, or your choice of breed. If you intend to leave your dog in daycare or to have him exercised by a professional dog walker, he may need to be neutered under the terms of your arrangement. If you are looking at a breed with a high risk of cancer, you might want to consider whether it is wise to neuter your dog at all. Golden Retrievers, for example, have a higher incidence of cancer than many other breeds and removing their sex hormones seems to make them particularly vulnerable, especially for females.

Differences in trainability between male and female dogs

When it comes to gender, male dogs seem to predominate in some sports. You could assume from this that males are more trainable, but in fact the reason is probably more to do with reproductive differences than with ability. We don't normally neuter our 'competition' dogs because, if successful, they will be expected to create the next generation of puppies. You can't compete with an in-season female as this would distract all the males in the competition, so entire female dogs are out of action, in a sporting context, for several weeks every time they come into season, and for even longer while they are pregnant and nursing puppies. It is pretty frustrating to have to withdraw a highly trained dog from an important competition because she comes into season a week or two early, so competing with a female dog is, for some people, less appealing.

When it comes to trainability, most people that have owned a lot of dogs of both sexes – people training Gundogs for competition, for example – will tell you that there is little difference between the sexes and that either can make wonderful pets. My own experience with Gundog breeds is that I have had very trainable female dogs and very trainable male dogs. I have also had more challenging dogs of both sexes. I have found both genders equally affectionate and happy to get along with people and other dogs.

Male or female summary

If you want to compete with your dog and won't be neutering, I suggest you consider buying a male to avoid your dog being out of action for several weeks each year. If you are definitely going to neuter your dog, you might want to avoid choosing a breed with a much higher than average incidence of cancer, or a breed where joint problems are a big issue – particularly in breeds where there are studies that have shown a correlation between neutering and these issues (for instance, Golden Retriever, Labradors, Hungarian Vizslas and German Shepherd Dogs). You can find notes on this topic, where relevant, in the Breed Reviews in Part Two.

Apart from that, there really is little to choose between male and female dogs. The chance of a male dog from a breed with known good temperament, bred from two good-tempered parents, being more or less aggressive or trainable than his sisters is slim. So go with your heart and pick the puppy that appeals to you.

Temperament and testing

While there are some broad generalisations that can be cautiously applied to different breeds, it is also true that, irrespective of gender, all dogs are individuals when it comes to temperament. There can be noticeable differences between two brothers from the same litter, for example; one may grow up to be more confident or more playful than another. It can be hard to be sure how much environment has played a part in these differences, but it is reasonable to assume that there is inherited variation between puppies of the same litter. So how are we supposed to detect these differences in puppies at just eight weeks old? Some breeders pin a lot of faith in some kind of temperament test in picking puppies. These tests can include things like observing a puppy's reaction to being touched in different ways, his response to sounds or novel objects and to being placed in an unfamiliar environment. However, such tests have always been controversial. And as Carole Beuchat from the Institute of Canine Biology advises on their website: 'Be very skeptical of claims that temperament can be assessed through evaluation of young puppies. If there is somebody who can reliably do this, they should document their success in a publication, because it would revolutionize the breeding of dogs.'

Temperament tests may be taken into account during the selection process for service dogs, but they are by no means foolproof and many dogs selected this way still fail to make the grade. So what does this tell you when it comes to choosing your puppy? I suggest you don't worry about subjecting him to a battery of tests. How well he 'performs' could simply be a feature of how tired he is that day or whether or not he has just had a meal.

The puppies' breeder may have noticed differences in personality between their puppies, by virtue of their experience, and the amount of time they have spent with the litter. But it is almost impossible for an outsider to make a reliable judgement of a puppy's character during a single visit. Obviously you should not consider buying a puppy that is clearly fearful or sick, but trying to identify small differences between puppies from a well-socialised and healthy litter is probably not effective, and your time would arguably be better spent talking to the breeder about the character of each puppy. In short, there is absolutely nothing wrong in picking a puppy simply because he rushed up to you or climbed into your lap. That's as good an indication as you're likely to get of a match made in heaven.

Differences in colour

I quite often hear people being dismissive of those that pick a puppy based on colour. But with certain provisos, I don't agree with this. Provided everything else is in place, in a healthy well-bred litter, there is nothing wrong with having a preference for one colour or another. However, there are a few colours that are associated with health issues and we should probably take a quick look at those.

White fur is associated with deafness in a number of different dog breeds. Various studies have found pigment associated deafness in some of our popular breeds, including the Cocker Spaniel, Bull Terrier, Whippet, Boxer, Dalmation, Border Collie, Cocker Spaniel, Bull Terrier, Whippet, and Jack Russell Terrier. That does *not* mean that all-white or partly white dogs *will* be deaf, but there is an increased risk of deafness in white or partly white puppies in these and some other dog breeds. White dogs can also be prone to sunburn.

Another colour that can cause problems is a dilute version of a standard colour. Blue or silver coats, for example, can be a diluted version of chocolate, and in some breeds the dilute gene is associated with a type of alopecia (baldness), together with skin inflammation, which can be quite severe. This is an issue in blue French Bulldogs, for example. Health problems are also associated with the merle gene (known as dapple in dachshunds). This is the gene that causes random patches of darker fur to lighten, and produces the attractive merle coat that we find in some breeds, like Border Collies. When a puppy inherits a single merle gene, together with a normal gene from the other parent, it usually results only in the attractive coat colour variation. But when a puppy inherits two copies of the merle gene, one from each parent, serious health problems, such as blindness, are common.

A good breeder will be aware of these issues. They will make good breeding choices, and will let you know of any potential problems with any particular puppy before you make *your* choice.

But, of course, not all breeders are equal. Let's have a quick look at some of the warning signs that tell you all is not well with the puppy in front of you.

Things to look out for and avoid

When you visit a litter of puppies at five or six weeks old, they should come tumbling out of their bed to greet you with wagging tails and enthusiasm. Don't just cuddle the puppies, observe how they behave on the ground. If you pick a puppy up and put him down in an unfamiliar place he may want to stay by your feet but he should not be paralysed with fear. In fact, none of these things should happen in a good litter:

- **Fearful trembling**
- **Puppy freezes or flattens himself to the ground**
- **Constantly crying puppy (pups may cry if they are too cold)**
- **Listless, lethargic puppy (not the same as sleepy)**
- **Smelly or dirty puppy.**

Remember that any puppy can step or roll in a poo just as visitors appear, and it is never possible to keep a whole litter squeaky clean all day. But puppies should not look 'grimy' or have a foul odour. Any of the above is a warning that you may need to review your choice of litter.

Physical examination

It is very difficult for anyone who is not experienced to physically examine a puppy and be certain that they are healthy. You can check your puppy's mouth to make sure his teeth are even and run your fingers over his tummy to check for umbilical hernias, but unless you know what you are doing, only the most obvious problems are likely to raise alarm bells. This is another reason why it is so important to get your choice of breeder and litter right in the first place.

If you are looking at puppies you have seen advertised, and don't know much about the breeder, it is important to take someone with you who has experience in handling and assessing puppies. Some puppies will have been vet checked before you visit. A vet check is a fairly brief physical examination of your puppy for obvious defects or signs of ill health, it is not an indication of future health. Not all breeders have puppies vet checked before leaving, and this does not indicate a lack of care. In any case, you should always have your puppy checked by your own vet within a day or two of arriving home.

What, no choice?

Let's now consider those situations where the puppy buyer has no choice at all. And this happens much more often than you might think – sometimes because all the other puppies are taken, and sometimes because the breeder insists on matching the individual puppies with the families he or she believes will suit them the best. If this happens to you, don't be downhearted. If you have chosen the breeder and litter carefully, all the puppies will be fantastic.

If you trust your breeder, and at this point you really should, and can't decide which puppy to take, a valid option is to let the breeder choose for you. Especially if he or she is experienced. The breeder knows their puppies better than anyone else, and stands a better chance of matching you with the dog whose personality suits you, than you do by stabbing in the dark.

Picking your puppy summary

I think the message here is that the overall choice of puppy in a well-chosen litter, should not be a big deal. Get the litter choice right, and pick the puppy that appeals to you most. If there is anything to take away from this chapter, it is 'don't sweat it'. Unless the puppy seems very fearful or nervous, pick the one you like the best and don't worry about the outcome. If all the scientists in the world can't predict a puppy's final temperament by testing it at eight weeks old, your chances of success are pretty slim. Far more important in determining the long-term future of your puppy are the choices you have made up to this point. You have done the hard work, now it's time to enjoy the results.
In the next and final chapter, you'll find plenty of additional resources to help you in your quest for the perfect puppy. Not everyone will want to purchase a puppy from one of the breeds reviewed in Part Two, so I'll give you the tools to do your own detective work and make an objective assessment of any breed of dog. I'll also leave you with a few final thoughts to help you on your journey.

4
Further Help and Information

C hoosing and raising a puppy is a huge emotional investment, as well as a financial one, and it's important that you make your investment wisely. Fashions in dog breeds come and go, but while popularity can sometimes indicate an easy temperament or trainability, it is rarely an indicator of health. Actively choosing a healthy breed is the first step in choosing and raising a healthy puppy. And as we have seen, it is not a straightforward process. We have looked at two big health issues for new puppy buyers to consider: structural problems and genetic problems.

Structural problems are more of an issue for *your* puppy because they often affect every single puppy in any given breed, to a greater or lesser extent. They are often ignored by breed clubs and breeders, who see them as 'normal' and don't consider them relevant. Structural defects can usually only be avoided entirely by choosing a different breed or crossbreed. Hopefully, with the information in this book, you will now be able to eliminate from your search those breeds with major disabilities built into the breed standard.

In the long term, genetic health is an issue of perhaps even greater importance for our pedigree breeds because of the problems we now know are associated with isolating small populations of animals. However, genetic health issues are something that puppy buyers can work around, to a certain extent, because modern science does at least provide us with tests for many of these conditions, provided we know what to look for. Ensuring that the parents of your puppy have all the relevant health clearances is crucial. You may feel a little awkward asking breeders for evidence, but this simple step can save a great deal of heartache in the future. Rest assured, all good breeders expect you to ask for certificates and will be happy to oblige.

✷ Choosing breeds not listed in the reviews

If you want to choose a breed not reviewed here, you'll need to do some detective work of your own. Check the structure of the dog first and foremost, and find out as much as you can about health problems in the breed. Extracting the relevant information from scientific papers can be challenging. Many scientific journals put their information behind a paywall, and a surprising number of breed clubs have little or no health information on their sites at all. Fortunately, most breeds have several clubs or associations, often with different clubs for different regions, and if you look at the websites for several of them you can often find what you need to know. A number of breeds have online databases, some of which contain a wealth of useful information for those looking for a puppy – you'll find these in the resources section at the end of this book. You can also find some useful information on the websites below.

The Kennel Club – www.thekennelclub.org.uk

The Kennel Club is the leading organisation representing dogs in the UK today. They do a great deal of good work for dogs through their charitable trust, and their website is a useful source of information. At the time of writing some of this information is rather scattered. You can find recommended tests for genetic problems under 'Breed Health' for each breed, but coefficients of inbreeding are in their own section. You then need to go to the 'Breed Watch' section to find information about structural health issues. In addition, not all breeds with severe structural problems are listed as 'cause for concern' under the Breed Watch scheme. Some of the data from the various KC/BVA health schemes is stored elsewhere – on the British Veterinary Association website, for example.

The Kennel Club also provides a list of breed clubs for each breed, which is a good starting point for your puppy search in any structurally sound breed. It is important, though, to be aware of the limitations of this information. For several of our disabled breeds, including French Bulldogs and Dachshunds, when you arrive on the website you might be forgiven for thinking that these physically compromised dogs do not have any health problems at all. This is because the Kennel Club's health information page for each breed is simply a list of recommended health tests. These pages don't cover health issues for which there are not tests, or which are inextricably linked to structure, such as brachycephalic obstructive airway syndrome (BOAS). This can be a little confusing for new puppy buyers because the picture they are being given of some breeds is incomplete.

There is no doubt that the Kennel Club is changing and improving. The information on genetic health is far better than it was ten years ago. But where structure is concerned, there is a good deal of catching up to do.

Dog Breed Health – www.dogbreedhealth.com

One website that is trying to bring important information together on one page for each of our pedigree breeds is the Dog Breed Health website. This website is designed specifically to help puppy buyers, and brings together both genetic information and information about the physical characteristics of each breed, including problems related to structure. It is a useful resource for anyone hoping to buy a pedigree puppy.

The Institute of Canine Biology – www.instituteofcaninebiology.org

I have mentioned The Institute of Canine Biology (ICB) quite a bit throughout this book. Their website is another good resource, packed with helpful information on various breeds, and the ICB is a huge force for good in the world of dog breeding. Unaffiliated with any kennel club, it runs courses for dog breeders and a series of Facebook groups for a variety of different breeds under their 'Breeding for The Future' programme. The idea is to bring breeders together in an educational environment and give them the skills they need to breed healthier dogs. If your puppy's breeder is a member of one of these groups, it is a promising sign that they are keen to learn and to help improve the health of their chosen breed.

The Happy Puppy Site – www.thehappypuppysite.com

I started The Happy Puppy Site in 2014 to provide information on finding and raising happy, healthy puppies. It is a companion to this book and you'll find many detailed breed reviews in addition to information on raising and training your puppy.

Dogs for special roles

If you want a dog for a particular role, it is often a good idea to look at the group of dogs that were originally bred for the purpose. Gundog breeds, unsurprisingly, tend to make good gundogs. Other breeds can be co-opted in, but you tend to get the best results if you stick to the original.

If you have allergies, a low-shedding dog such as the Miniature Schnauzer or the Poodle is probably a good choice. Bear in mind that some people with allergies still react to low-shedding or supposedly 'non-shedding' breeds. Many crossbreeds where one parent is low-shedding and the other is *not* are a gamble because not all the puppies will be non-shedding. A Labradoodle litter, for example, may well include some low-shedding puppies *and* some heavily-shedding ones. Bear in mind, also, that low-shedding breeds often have high maintenance, continually growing, coats that need a lot of grooming.

Raising your puppy

Bringing home a puppy with a chance of a long and healthy life is just the start. You'll want to do everything you can to ensure that he stays fit and healthy for many years to come. You can find plenty of help and advice in my book *The Happy Puppy Handbook*, which will take you through the first few months of life at home with a brand new puppy. But one simple thing you can do, which more than anything else will help your puppy to stay well, is to keep him slim. The large 2004 health survey referenced throughout this book discovered that the age of death in dogs is significantly negatively correlated with ideal bodyweight. This means the fatter your dog gets, the shorter his life will be compared to other dogs of his breed. The message here is clear; if you want to enjoy your dog's company for the longest time, keep him slim.

The future for dogs

While we can improve the odds of *your* puppy having a long and healthy life, the future for pedigree dogs as a whole is uncertain. Over the last ten years, dogs from the Working group and Terriers have lost half their annual registration numbers. Pastoral dogs have declined by one third, and Gundogs by one fifth. Only the Utility dogs have grown in popularity, and that growth is fuelled almost entirely by the interest in brachycephalic breeds. Such a catastrophic fall in numbers is very bad for isolated groups of dogs, and many breeds are now 'at risk' of extinction. Once lost, genetic material can never be recovered.

This puts pedigree dogs between a rock and a hard place. Genetic diversity together with a healthy population size are essential for the long-term survival of any group of animals, but the only dogs where we are seeing improvements in this respect are the brachycephalic breeds such as Pugs and Bulldogs – a group of dogs so badly structured that life is 'at best' uncomfortable for them. Reading about all this is often uncomfortable for us, too, and it is tempting to simply brush it aside. It is very hard when you have your heart set on a particular breed to hear about the kind of health problems that may befall your future friend. It would have been easy to have written this book as a bright and breezy guide to puppies, full of puppy pictures and happy descriptions of the qualities of each of our popular breeds, with no emphasis at all on the real problems that exist within them, but I could not in all conscience ignore this opportunity to help raise awareness of the impact of current breeding practices on our wonderful companions.

Genetic diversity

Many population biologists and geneticists fear that our pedigree breeds will be lost forever if outcrossing is not widely implemented, and soon. This means we must consider matings between dogs from different breeds. Unfortunately, there is a profound fear among those that consider themselves 'guardians of our dog breeds', the breeders themselves, of losing the 'purity' of each individual breed. This fear is a tremendous barrier to progress when it comes to saving our pedigree gene pools. Of course, it is entirely possible to introduce controlled outcrossing on a regular basis without losing the qualities and characteristics of the breeds we love, but this message is either not being received by dog breeders, or it is being received and rejected, and there seems little enthusiasm for enforcing a solution on them. Perhaps influencing those who control such matters is outside my power and yours. Where we do have some say is in insisting that our *own* puppies are given a good start by providing them with a healthy body to carry them through life.

A healthy puppy is a happy puppy

Perhaps I can leave you with this thought. The further we move away from the blueprint that is the grey wolf, the greater the risk of structural problems in our dogs. And dogs really do need that sound body structure. It is a fundamental prerequisite for running, jumping, climbing and swimming, and all the other activities that should come naturally to our four-legged friends. When we interfere with the biomechanics of the dog by introducing various forms of dwarfism, or when we interfere with the way the dog cools and oxygenates himself, by breeding from dogs with genetically shortened faces, we give our puppies a much increased risk of truly horrible problems – back pain, difficulty breathing, distressing eye infections and a good deal more. Puppies are being produced with these disabilities because people are buying them. This is something you can make a choice over.

There is much in life that we can't control, but giving each new puppy a sound body to carry him around for the next ten years or more is firmly within our grasp. Insisting on a well-constructed, healthy dog will do far more than help secure a long and happy life for your best friend. It will help to give dogs around the world a brighter future.

🐾 Resources

Books by the author

Total Recall: Perfect Response Training for Puppies and Adult Dogs (Quiller, 2012)

The Happy Puppy Handbook: Your Definitive Guide to Puppy Care and Early Training (Ebury, 2014)

The Labrador Handbook: The definitive guide to training and caring for your Labrador (Ebury, 2015)

Useful websites

1. Animal Health Trust: www.aht.org.uk
2. British Veterinary Association: bva.co.uk
3. Cocker Spaniel Database: www.cockerspanieldatabase.info
4. Dog Bite Statistics: www.dogsbite.org
5. Dog Breed Health: www.dogbreedhealth.com
6. The Happy Puppy Site: thehappypuppysite.com
7. The Institute of Canine Biology: www.instituteofcaninebiology.org
8. Kennel Club Pure Breed Health Survey 2004: www.thekennelclub.org.uk/vets-researchers/purebred-breed-health-survey-2004/
9. Kennel Club Pedigree Breed Health Survey 2014: www.thekennelclub.org.uk/vets-researchers/pedigree-breed-health-survey-2014
10. Kennel Club Inbreeding coefficient calculator: www.thekennelclub.org.uk/services/public/mateselect/inbreed/Default.aspx
11. The Labrador Site: www.thelabradorsite.com
12. Orthopedic Foundation for Animals: www.offa.org
13. Universities Federation for Animal Welfare: www.ufaw.org.uk
14. University of Sydney, List of disorders by breed: sydney.edu.au/vetscience/research/disorders/companion/lida.shtml
15. World Small Animal Veterinary Association: www.wsava.org

References

Brachycephaly

1. Fasanella, F.J., Shivley, J.M., Wardlaw, J.L. and Givaruangsawat, S., 'Brachycephalic airway obstructive syndrome in dogs: 90 cases (199-2008)'. *Journal of the American Veterinary Medical Association* 237, 9 (2010): 1048–51
2. Packer, R.M.A, Hendricks, A., Tivers, M.S. and Burn, C.C. 'Impact of Facial Conformation on Canine Health: Brachycephalic Obstructive Airway Syndrome'. *PLoS ONE* 10, 10 (2015): e0137496
3. Trappler, M. and Moor, K.W., 'Canine Brachycephalic Airway Syndrome: Pathophysiology, Diagnosis, and Nonsurgical Management'. *Compendium* 33, 5 (2011)

Behaviour

1. Akkad, D.A., Gerding, W.M., Gasser, R.B. and Epplen, J.T., 'Homozygosity mapping and sequencing identify two genes that might contribute to pointing behavior in hunting dogs'. *Canine Genetic and Epidemiology* 2, 5 (2015)
2. Duffy, D.L., Yuying, H. and Serpell, J.A., 'Breed differences in canine aggression'. *Applied Animal Behaviour Science* 114, 3–4 (2008): 441–60

3. Pirrone, F., Pierantoni, L., Quintavalle Pastorino, G. and Albertini, M., 'Owner-reported aggressive behaviour towards familiar people may be more prominent occurrence in pet shop-traded dogs'. *Journal of Veterinary Behavior: Clinical Applications and Research* 11 (2015): 13–17

4. Sacks, J.J., Sinclair, L., Gilchrist, J., Golab, G.C. and Lockwood, R., 'Breeds of dogs involved in fatal human attacks in the United States between 1979 and 1998'. *Journal of the American Veterinary Medical Association* 217, 6 (200): 836–40

5. Spady, T.C. and Ostrander, E.A., 'Canine Behavioral Genetics: Pointing Out the Phenotypes and Herding up the Genes'. *The American Journal of Human Genetics* 82, 1 (2008): 10–18

6. Stone, H.R., McGreevy, P.D., Starling, M.J. and Forkman, B., 'Associations between Domestic-Dog Morphology and Behaviour Scores in the Dog Mentality Assessment'. *PLoS ONE* 11, 2 (2016): e0149403

Breed studies

1. Beardow, A.W. and Buchanan, J.W., 'Chronic mitral valve disease in Cavalier King Charles Spaniels: 95 cases (1987–1991)'. *Journal of the American Veterinary Medical Association* 203, 7 (1993): 1023–9

2. Bhalerao, D.P., Rajpurohit, Y., Vite, C.H. and Giger, U., 'Detection of genetic mutation of myotonia congenital among Miniature Schnauzers and identification of a common carrier ancestor'. *American Journal of Veterinary Research* 63, 10 (2002): 1443–7

3. Black, V., Garosi, L., Lowrie, M., Harvey, R.J. and Gale, J., 'Phenotypic characterisation of canine epileptoid cramping syndrome in the Border Terrier'. *Journal of Small Animal Practice* 55, 2 (2014)

4. Mitchell, T.J., Knowler, S.P., van den Berg, H., Sykes, J. and Rusbridge, C., 'Syringomyelia: determining risk and protective factors in the conformation of the Cavalier King Charles Spaniel dog'. *Canine Genetics and Epidemiology* 1, 9 (2014)

5. Nowend, et al., 'Characterization of the Genetic Basis for Autosomal Recessive Hereditary Nephropathy in the English Springer Spaniel'. *Journal of Veterinary Internal Medicine* 26 (2012): 294–301

6. Summers, J.F., O'Neill, D.G., Church, D.B., Thompson, P.C., McGreevy, P.D. and Brodbelt, D.C., 'Prevalence of disorders recorded in Cavalier King Charles Spaniels attending primary-care veterinary practices in England'. *Canine Genetics and Epidemiology* 2, 4 (2015)

Coat colour and deafness

1. Platt, S., Freeman, J., Di Stefani, A., Wieczorek, L. and Henley, W., 'Prevalence of unilateral and bilateral deafness in border collies and association with phenotype'. *Journal of Veterinary Internal Medicine* 20, 6 (2006):1355–62

2. Strain, G.M., 'Deafness prevalence and pigmentation and gender associations in dog breeds at risk'. *The Veterinary Journal* 167, 1 (2004): 23–32

3. Strain, G.M., Clark, L.A., Wahl, J.M., Turner, A.E. and Murphy, K.E., 'Prevalence of deafness in dogs heterozygous or homozygous for the merle allele'. *Journal of Veterinary Internal Medicine* 23, 2 (2009): 282 6

Dermatitis and allergies

1. Griffin, C.E., 'Skin immune system and allergic diseases'. in *Muller and Kirk's Small Animal Dermatology*. (Saunders, 2001)

2. Jackson, H.A., 'Dermatologic manifestations and nutritional management of adverse food reactions'. *Veterinary Medicine* (January 2007): 51–64

3. Shaw, S.C., Wood, J.L.N., Freeman, J., Littlewood, J.D. and Hannant, D., 'Estimation of heritability of atopic dermatitis in Labrador and Golden Retrievers'. *American Journal of Veterinary Research* 65, 7 (2004): 1014–20

Fashions and popularity

1. Ghirlanda, S., Acerbi, A. and Herzog, H. 'Dog Movie Stars and Dog Breed Popularity: A Case Study in Media Influence on Choice'. *PLoS ONE* 9, 9 (2014): e106565

2. Ghirlanda, S., Acerbi, A., Herzog, H. and Serpell, J.A., 'Fashion vs. Function in Cultural Evolution: The Case of Dog Breed Popularity'. *PLoS ONE* 8, 9 (2013): e74770

3. Herzog, H., 'Forty-two Thousand and One Dalmatians: Fads, Social Contagion, and Dog Breed Popularity'. *Society & Animals* 14, 4 (2006): 383–97

4. Keating, C.F., Randall, D.W., Kendrick, T. and Gutshall, K.A., 'Fashion and the appeal of neoteny'. *Journal of Non Verbal Behaviour* 27, (2003): 89–109

5. Murray, J.K., Browne, W.J., Roberts, M.A., Whitmarsh, A. and Gruffydd-Jones, T.J., 'Number and ownership profiles of cats and dogs in the UK'. *Veterinary Record* 166 (2010): 163–8

Genetics and inherited diseases

1. Dobson, J.M., 'Breed-Predispositions to Cancer in Pedigree Dogs'. *ISRN Veterinary Science* 2013 (2013): Article 941275

2. Gresky, C., Hamann, H. and Distl, O., 'Influence of inbreeding on litter size and the proportion of stillborn puppies in dachshunds'. *Berliner und Münchener Tierärztliche Wochenschrift* 118, 3–4 (2005), 134–9

3. Van Rooy, D., Arnott, E.R., Early, J.B., McGreevy, P. and Wade, C.M., 'Holding back the genes: limitations of research into canine behavioural genetics'. *Canine Genetics and Epidemiology* 1, 7 (2014)

Health surveys and longevity

1. Adams, V.J., Evans, K.M., Sampson, J. and Wood, J.L.N., 'Methods and mortality results of a health survey of purebred dogs in the UK'. *Journal of Small Animal Practice* 51, 10 (2010): 512–24

2. Dobson, J., Hoather, T., McKinley, T.J. and Wood, J.L., 'Mortality in a cohort of flat-coated retrievers in the UK'. *Veterinary and Comparative Oncology* 7, 2 (2009): 115–21

3. Egenvall, A., Bonnett, B.N., Hedhammar, A. and Olson, P., 'Mortality in over 350,000 Insured Swedish Dogs from 1995—2000: II. Breed-Specific Age and Survival Patterns and Relative Risk for Causes of Death'. *Acta Veterinaria Scandinavica* 46, 3 (2005): 121–36

4. Egenvall, A., Bonnett, B.N., Hedhammar, A. and Olson, P., 'Gender, age, breed and distribution of morbidity and mortality in insured dogs in Sweden during 1995 and 1996'.

5. Farrell, L.L., Schoenebeck, J.J., Wiener, P., Clements, D.N. and Summers, K.M., 'The challenges of pedigree dog health: approaches to combating inherited disease'. *Canine Genetics and Epidemiology* 2, 3 (2015)

6. Michell, A.R., 'Longevity of British breeds of dog and its relationships with sex, size, cardiovascular variables and disease'. *Veterinary Record* 145, 22 (1999): 625–9

7. O'Neill, D.G., Church, D.B., McGreevy, P.D., Thomson, P.C. and Brodbelt, D.C., 'Prevalence of Disorders Recorded in Dogs Attending Primary-Care Veterinary Practices in England'. *PLoS ONE* 9, 3 (2014): e90501, *Veterinary Record* 146 (2000): 519–25

8. O'Neill, D.G., Church, D.B., McGreevy, P.D., Thomson, P.C. and Brodbelt, D.C., 'Longevity and mortality of owned dogs in England'. *Veterinary Journal* 198, 3 (2013): 638–43

9. Proschowsky, H.F., Rugbjerg, H., and Ersboll, A.K., 'Mortality of purebred and mixed-breed dogs in Denmark'. *Preventive Veterinary Medicine* 58, 1–2 (2003): 63–74

Joint health

1. Impellizeri, J.A., Tetrick, M.A. and Muir, P., 'Effect of weight reduction on clinical signs of lameness in dogs with hip osteoarthritis'. *Journal of the American Veterinary Medical Association* 216, 7 (2000): 1089–91

2. Krontveit, R.I., Nodtvedt, A., Saevik, B.K., Ropstad, E. and Trangerud, C., 'Housing – and exercise-related risk factors associated with the development of hip dysplasia as determined by radiographic evaluation in a prospective cohort of Newfoundlands, Labrador Retrievers, Leonbergers, and Irish Wolfhounds in Norway'. *American Journal of Veterinary Research* 73, 6 (2012): 838–46

3. Lewis, T.W., Blott, S.C. and Wooliams, J.A., 'Genetic Evaluation of Hip Score in UK Labrador Retrievers'. *PLoS ONE* 5, 10 (2010): e12797

4. Manley, P.A., Adams, W.M., Danielson, K.C., Tass Dueland, R., Linn, K.A., 'Long-term outcome of juvenile pubic symphysiodesis and triple pelvic osteotomy in dogs with hip dysplasia'. *Journal of the American Veterinary Medical Association*. 230, 2 (2007): 206–10

5. O'Neill, D.G., Meeson, R.L., Sheridan, A., Church, D.B. and Brodbelt, D.C., 'The epidemiology of patellar luxation in dogs attending primary-care veterinary practices in England'. *Canine Genetics and Epidemiology* 3, 4 (2016)

6. Paster, E.R., LaFond, E., Biery, D., Iriye, A., Gregor, T.P., Shofer, F.S. and Smith, G.K., 'Estimates of prevalence of hip dysplasia in Golden Retrievers and Rottweilers and the influence of bias on published prevalence figures'. *Journal of the American Veterinary Medical Association* 226, 3 (2005): 387–92

7. Smith, G.K., Paster, E.R., Powers, M.Y., Lawler, D.F., Biery, D.N., Shofer, F.S., McKelvie, P.J. and Kealy, R.D., 'Lifelong diet restriction and radiographic evidence of osteoarthritis of the hip joint in dogs'. *Journal of the American Veterinary Medical Association* 229, 5 (2006): 690–93

8. van Hagen, M.A.E., Ducro, B.J., van den Broek, J. and Knol, B.W., 'Incidence, risk factors, and heritability estimates of hind limb lameness caused by hip dysplasia in a birth cohort of Boxers'. *American Journal of Veterinary Research* 66, 2 (2005): 307–12

9. Witsberger, T.H., Villamil, J.A., Schultz, L.G., Hahn, A.W., Cook, J.L., 'Prevalence of and risk factors for hip dysplasia and cranial cruciate ligament deficiency in dogs'. *Journal of the American Veterinary Medical Association* 232, 12 (2008), 1818–24

Intervertebral disc disease

1. Bull., C., Fehr, M. and Tipold, A., 'Canine intervertebral disk disease: a retrospective study of clinical outcome in 238 dogs'. *Berliner und Münchener Tierärztliche Wochenschrift* 121, 3–4 (2008): 159–70

2. Ghosh, P., 'The role of mechanical and genetic factors in degeneration of the disc'. *J Manual Med* 5 (1990): 62–5

3. Jensen, V.F. and Arnbjerg, J., 'Development of intervertebral disk calcification in the dachshund: a prospective longitudinal radiographic study'. *Journal of the American Animal Association* 37, 3 (2001): 274–82

4. Jensen, V., Beck, S., Christensen, K. and Ambjerg, J., 'Quantification of the association between intervertebral disc calcification and disc herniation in Dachshunds'. *Journal of the American Veterinary Medical Association* 233, 7 (2008): 1090–5

5. Levine, J., Levine, G., Kerwin, S., Hettlich, B. and Fosgate, G., 'Association between various physical factors and acute thoracolumbar intervertebral disc extrusion or protrusion in Dachshunds'. *Journal of the American Veterinary Medical Association* 229. 3 (2006): 370–5

6. Packer, R.M.A., Hendricks, A., Holger, A.V., Shihab, N.K. and Burn, C.C., 'How Long and Low Can You Go? Effect of Conformation on the Risk of Thoracolumbar Intervertebral Disc Extrusion in Domestic Dogs'. *PLoS ONE* 8, 7 (2013): e69650

Neutering and its effects on health

1. Cooley, D.M., Beranek, B.C., Schlittler, D.L., Glickman, N.W., Glickman, L.T. and Waters. D.J., 'Endogenous gonadal hormone exposure and bone sarcoma risk'. *Cancer Epidemiology, Biomarkers & Prevention* 11, 11 (2002): 1434–40

2. Hart, B.L., Hart, L.A., Thigpen, A.P. and Willits, N.H., 'Long-Term Health Effects of Neutering Dogs: Comparison of Labrador Retrievers with Golden Retrievers'. *PLoS ONE* 9, 7 (2014): e102241

3. Hart, B.L., Hart, L.A., Thigpen, A.P. and Willits, N.H., 'Neutering of German Shepherd Dogs: associated joint disorders, cancers and urinary incontinence'. *Veterinary Medicine and Science* (2016)

4. Torres de la Riva, G., Hart, B.L., Farver, T.B., Oberbauer, A.M., McV Messam, L.L., Willits, N. and Hart, L.A., 'Neutering Dogs: Effects on joint disorders and cancers in Golden Retrievers'. *PLoS One* 8 2 (2013): e55937

5. Zink, M.C., Farhoody, P., Elser, S.E., Ruffini, L.D., Gibbons, T.A. and Rieger, R.H., 'Evaluation of the risk and age of onset of cancer and behavioural disorders in gonadectomized Vizslas'. *Journal of the American Veterinary Medical Association* 244, 3 (2014): 309–19

Index